RICHARD GRIFFITH

AND

HIS VALUATIONS OF IRELAND

with

AN INVENTORY OF THE BOOKS OF THE
GENERAL VALUATION OF RATEABLE PROPERTY IN IRELAND

Conducted under 9 & 10 Vict. c. 110 of 1846 and 15 & 16 Vict. c. 63 of 1852

by

James R. Reilly
Board Certified Genealogical Records Specialist

CLEARFIELD

Printed for
Clearfield Company, Inc. by
Genealogical Publishing Co., Inc.
Baltimore, Maryland
2000

Reprinted for
Clearfield Company, Inc. by
Genealogical Publishing Co., Inc.
Baltimore, Maryland
2001, 2002

International Standard Book Number: 0-8063-4954-9

Made in the United States of America

To the memory of

John R. Ruane

The Founding President of The Irish Family History Forum

Contents

VII. FIGURES

Acknowledgments

It has been almost a hundred and fifty years since Sir Richard Griffith completed his monumental undertaking of valuing the island of Ireland to secure an unbiased and equitable tax base for the wealthy and the poor alike.

This manual hopefully will assist researchers to gain a comprehensive understanding of his work and to use it to achieve a fuller perception of their ancestors.

Judy Wight AG, a dear friend and staff member of the LDS Family History Library and who is an internationally recognized author and lecturer about Irish research, proposed revisions that enhanced my material.

Kyle Betit and Dwight Radford, whose *The Irish At Home and Abroad* is a renowned leader in scholarly Irish research, contributed invaluable suggestions to improve my manuscript's content and presentation.

Diane Loosle AG, Family History Library British Isles staff member, offered advice based on her experience with Library patrons.

Special recognition is due to the individuals and institutions named here who shared and supported the compiler's belief in the need for an inventory of Sir Richard Griffith's monumental accomplishment. The boundless gifts of personal time and gentle solicitude extended by each woman and man enabled me during my extended research in their repositories to complete the An Inventory of the Books of Sir Richard Griffith's General Valuation of Rateable Property in Ireland. They will be remembered and extolled within our mutual research community for their unselfish assistance: Patrick Scanlon of the Valuation Office; Director David Craig and Archivist Aideen Ireland of the National Archives of Ireland; Archives staff member Ken Robinson at the Four Courts; Dr. Maire Kennedy, senior librarian of the Dublin Gilbert Library; Kevin Brown, senior administrative officer of the National Library and staff member Noel Brady; and the staffs of the county libraries for their professional support.

INTRODUCTION

Although acknowledged by genealogists as an invaluable census substitute for mid-nineteenth century Ireland, much of the history of Richard Griffith's monumental work in the field of land valuation is unknown. What is commonly referred to as "Griffith's Valuation" is actually the last of three valuations conducted by him, the first of which had its beginnings in 1825.

Richard Griffith, born in Dublin in 1784, was the son of a distinguished member of Parliament. At age fifteen he was sent to Cornwall in England to study mining but obtained a commission in the Royal Artillery in 1799. After two years of service, he resigned his commission to begin the study of geology and mineralogy at Edinburgh University in Scotland. After several years of study, he began a life-long career of government service in 1808 when he undertook an extensive study of bog drainage in Ireland for the House of Commons. In 1812 the Royal Dublin Society decided to appoint a mining engineer. In appointing Richard John Griffith, the Society brought into its service one of the most gifted Irishmen of his time. He served as Inspector of Irish Mines and superintended road construction in southwest Ireland from 1822 until 1839. With his appointment as Boundary Surveyor in 1825, he began a career in land valuation that was to span forty years. Sir Richard was created a baronet in 1858.[1]

By the early years of the nineteenth century, two structures of local taxation in Ireland had become a long-standing source of contention among the country's tax-paying population. The tithe, a tax equivalent to ten percent in kind of the agricultural produce of a rural piece of land, was collected regardless of the occupier's religious denomination by the ecclesiastical authority of the state Church of Ireland for the support of its clergy. The 'county cess'[2] was imposed by the civil authority of each county's 'grand jury' for the construction and repair of roads and to meet expenses in connection with courthouses, county infirmaries and fever hospitals, and lunatic asylums.

The county cess was levied on land occupiers, whether owner, 'middleman,' or 'tenant,' by a charge assessed on the ancient territorial division known in most parts of Ireland as 'townland.' Each grand jury's unique system of determining the acreage of a townland and the proportional share of the county cess to be imposed upon each occupier caused problems. There were frequent complaints that a townland's acreage and taxable value were subject to prejudiced and inequitable practices by the local assessors who were suspected of basing their valuation on their friendship with landlords or under social pressure exerted on them.

To eliminate these inequities, landowners and tenants sought a country-wide uniform system of land measuring and valuing to be managed by a centralized Irish government authority. The initial

---

[1] Mary Olive Hussey, "Sir Richard Griffith, The Man and His Work," *Dublin Historical Review* 20 (1965).
[2] Terms enclosed in a single quotation mark are defined in Appendix No.1.

step to achieve that system was taken in 1825 with the establishment of the Boundary Department of Ireland with Richard Griffith at its head under the authority of 6 Geo. IV, Cap. 99. ("Geo. IV, Cap. 99" translates into "The 99th Chapter of the Statutes enacted by Parliament in the Sixth Year of the Reign of King George the Fourth.")

Figure 1. Sir Richard Griffith
National Library of Ireland

THE BOUNDARY AND ORDNANCE SURVEYS

Although the name and configuration of a townland were known to local tax assessors, its precise acreage in some sections of the country was not known because units of measure other than 'acre' were used that had little or no relationship to land area. For example, the unit of measure in Kerry, Cork and Waterford was the "ploughland," in Cavan the "carvagh," in Fermanagh the "tate."[3] In addition, the problem was compounded by measuring land in either English stature acres or Irish acres, substantially different measures. Consequently, cases of extreme discrepancy in valuation had been reported by taxpayers to the various parliamentary committees investigating taxation methods between 1815 and 1824. The common people were especially angry because they bore the brunt of these inequitable systems. As a preliminary step to a detailed valuation of land and buildings, Parliament had required that every grand jury prepare for each barony within its county a list of the "Names of the several Parishes, Townlands, Manors, Ploughlands, or other Divisions or Sub-divisions or Sub-denominations" with their acreage or, if not acreage, the"Mode or Manner in which the Cess has been levied."[4]

Two projects had to be undertaken before a boundary survey and a property valuation could commence. First, marking the boundaries commonly accepted by grand juries, landowners and tenants of every townland, civil parish and barony in a county; this responsibility was assigned to Richard Griffith and his new Boundary Department. Second, undertaking a scientific topographical survey of these land divisions; this responsibility was assigned to Lieutenant Colonel Thomas Colby and to the Royal Engineers and Royal Artillery.

Assigned to follow in the wake of Griffith's men who were marking boundaries, military personnel, called Ordnance Survey teams each led by a lieutenant, were to survey the major land divisions. Skilled and experienced in the creation of maps used by the British Army, the Engineers were the logical choice to undertake the making of topographical maps for use in time by Griffith's valuators in the implementation of the future valuation of land, buildings and other fixed property. Although the minutely accurate acreage figures required by Griffith's valuators was a task for which the Ordnance officers had not been specifically trained, Colby instructed his men to meticulously measure the acreage and to ensure that the roads, houses and other details inside the boundaries were measured with more exactitude than would have been considered appropriate in a purely military context.

---

[3] J.H. Andrews, *A Paper Landscape: The Ordnance Survey in Nineteenth Century Ireland* (Oxford: Clarendon Press, 1975), p. 119.
[4] 6 Geo. IV., Cap. 99, Section III.

Figure 2. Thomas Colby
Ordnance Survey Office

Figure 3. John O'Donovan
National Gallery of Ireland

Beginning with the list of townlands obtained from the high constable of each barony, Griffith checked townland names with local landowners and the local incumbents of the Church of Ireland. Where necessary he used local estate maps to refine boundaries, and in some cases he laid out completely new boundaries for tracts of bog and mountain that had not previously been part of any townland. Accompanied by an Ordnance officer, two enlisted men and a hired local resident, called a "meresman," to assist in indentifying the boundaries, Griffith's field staff would walk the reputed boundary of a townland marking it with posts, blocks of wood or stone, and marks on houses, trees or posts. Exact notes of bearings and distances were recorded by the Ordnance officer in a "boundary register." By direction of Lord Wellington, the British prime minister, the topographical maps to be drawn after the "walk about" were to be on a scale of six inches to one statute mile, thereby making them large enough to show clearly and accurately a townland's boundaries.[5] They were to show houses, streams, rivers, fences, and trees. The subsequent Ordnance Survey documents, 3170 maps and 2306 boundary registers, are divided between the Dublin National Archives and the Belfast Public Record Office.

---

[5] J.H. Andrews, *A Paper Landscape: The Ordnance Survey in Nineteenth-Century Ireland* (Oxford: Clarendon Press, 1975), p.12.

Figure 4. Ordnance Boundary Survey Register Page, Co. Mayo,
Parish of Aghamore, Kilgariff Townland.
National Archives of Ireland

From the point described in page (6) where the Townlands of Larganboy West in the Parish of Bekan Kilgariff and Coogay South in Aughamore Parish meet the Boundary between the two latter Townlands proceeds SW with centre of wall 4 chs (chains) 13 links. There a fence joins from the SW, Bog commences on the same side and the Boundary proceeds with top of bank in same direction 1 ch to a mound. Here the Bog commences on the NE and the Boundary proceeds through the same undefined in the same NW direction 11 chs on [?] a mound and 7 1/2 chs farther meets another on the SE side of a lane or bye Road which the Boundary crosses for 60 links and proceeds West with centre of drain through Bog 9 1/4 chs to a mound. Here the boundary leaves the drain and proceeds at undefined 6 1/2 chs to a mound. Here the Boundary turns NW with the top of bank 1 1/2 chs on a fence going from the WSW at a point 1 1/2 chs W of a Fort and the Boundary continues as described 74 chs on a fence joins from the SSE [?]   ). 6 chs farther the Bog ceases. 2 chs on the Boundary being W 1 3/4 chs where it joins the E side of a lane. Here the Townlands of Kilgariff Coogay South and Coogay Middle meet.

Figure 5. Transcription of Ordnance Survey Boundary Register, Co. Mayo
Parish of Aghamore, Kilgariff Townland.

In Figure 6 the heavy black lines are the townland boundaries of Pottlebane and its adjoining townlands surveyed by the Ordnance Survey team in 1836. The fine lines within the townland mark the boundaries of the individual tenements, each showing the number assigned to it by a surveyor in 1854.

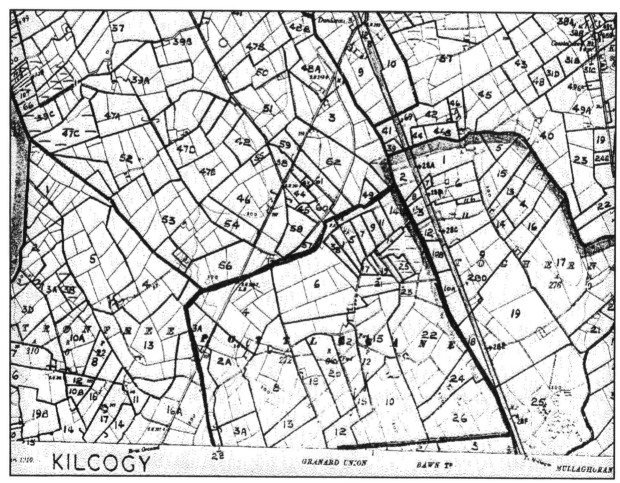

Figure 6. Section of 6 Inch-to-a-Mile Ordnance Survey Map, Townland of Pottlebane,
Parish of Drumlumman, Co. Cavan
Valuation Office

When the boundaries were "sufficiently ascertained" by the team, the Act stipulated that the penalty for defacing, destroying, or mutilating any such marking was £2 to £10 should any occupier surreptitiously question Griffith's demarcation.[6] It is not surprising that in the first year there were some 6000 legal challanges by landholders to his demarcations.

After some early difficulties in Co. Londonderry, the first county to have its barony, parish and townland boundaries identified, Griffith decided to supply the Ordnance officer with "sketch maps" to supplement the boundary information given by the meresmen. The sketches, not to be confused with the technical maps prepared by the Ordnance teams, were drawn with surprising accuracy according to Colby[7]; they detail streams, roads, buildings and prehistoric earthworks. Genealogists should be aware that an examination of Griffith's boundary sketches may show occupier names recorded for some of the houses shown on the sketches. Occupier names "Patt McDonnell, Peter Martin, Peter Rooney, Widow Carroll, John Crawley, Philip Malone," for example, appear on the sketch of the parish of Charlestown in Co. Louth drawn on 28 November 1828. McDonnell, Rooney, Carroll and Crawley surnames occupying moderate sized holdings continue to appear in an 1854 valuation of Charlestown. A large collection of the boundary sketches is available at the National Archives of Ireland.

In most cases Colby adopted the townland names supplied to Griffith by a grand jury. Although Griffith had made a great effort to obtain the authentic versions of the names, Colby preferred to create his own system by supplying his surveyors with a printed "Name Book" to record each townland's name as commonly spelled and its various deviant spellings citing the source for each spelling. The sources noted in the Name Book included local government records, estate papers, clergymen and local residents. A remarks column recorded notes on soils, farming practices, leases and rents, prominent buildings, the social condition of the people, and the most common surnames in the townland.[8]

Pottlebaun	
Poiteal Bån	*White pottle of land*
POTTLEBAN	*J O'Donovan*
POTTLEBAW	*Boundary Survey Sketch Map*
POTTLEBAU	*County Map*
POTTLEBAUN	*Barony Map*
POTTLEBAWN	*Tithe Commissioners*
POTTLEBAWN	*Grand Jury List 1824*

[4] 6 Geo. IV, Cap. 99, Section, Section XII.
[7] Andrews, *A Paper Landscape*, p.12.
[8] Ibid, p. 16.

> *Contains 271 statute acres. 36 of which are bog. The property of the Marquis of Westmeath. No leases. Rent from £1.10 to £1.12 per Irish acre. Bog rent 10s per Irish acre. Soil of a light sandy nature. Produces oats, flax, and potatoes. The main road from Granard to Ballynagh runs through the N.W. part of the townland.*

Figure 7. Transcription of typescript, *Co. Cavan Name Books*, Drumlomann Parish, Vol. 2, p. 43
National Library of Ireland

Irish scholar John O'Donovan was employed to recommend standard Irish forms of townland names. He was sent to the areas being surveyed to talk, where possible, with Irish speaking residents to learn the Irish forms of townland names. Typescripts of some Name Books can be viewed at the National Library of Ireland.

While there is limited genealogical information contained in Boundary Survey documents, the fact that they contain names of landowners, geographical subdivisions and subdenominations of townlands may help the researcher identify an illusive or unfamiliar place-name of an ancestor found in family documents or oral tradition.

The Ordnance Survey Townland Index Map

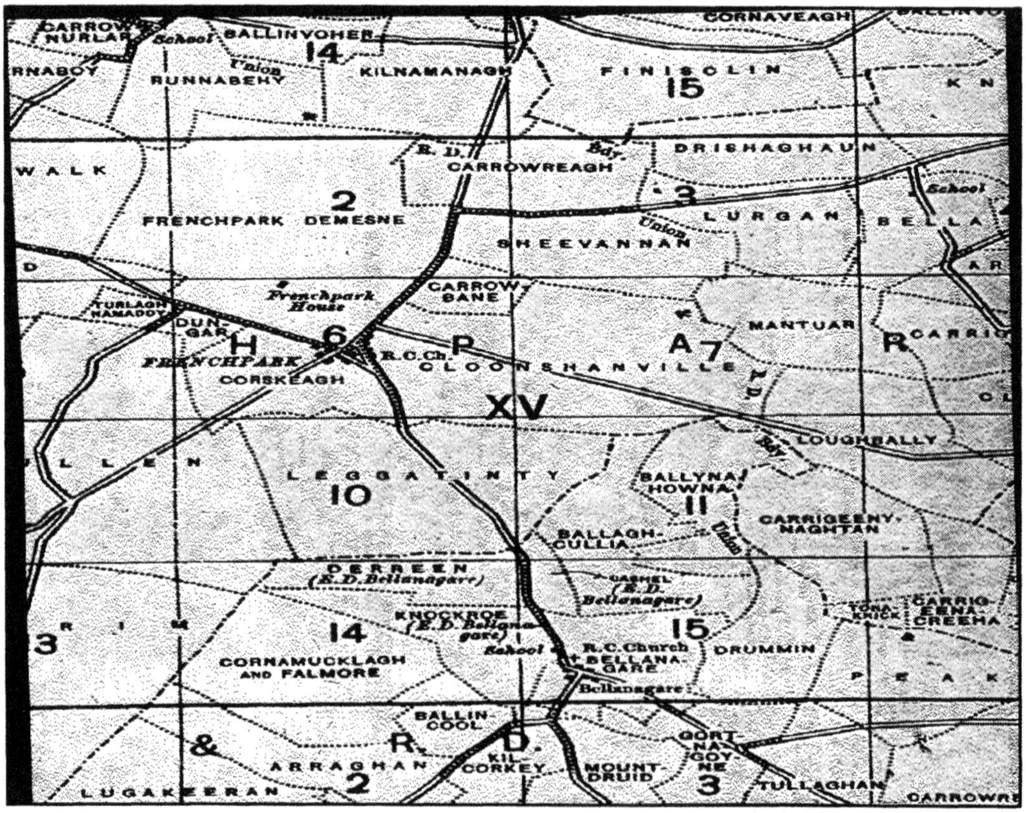

Figure 8. Townland Index Map, Co. Roscommon. Dotted lines represent townland boundaries, dash-and-dotted lines are barony boundaries. Six-inch sheets are shown by roman numeral; arabic numbers represent one-inch-to-a-mile sheets. Ordnance Survey Office

The "Townland Index Map" is a series of maps undertaken in 1909 by the Ordnance Survey Office to index the original 6" OS maps. Based on a scale of one inch to the mile, the index maps show the boundary of townlands and include a useful selection of roads, railways, major rivers and public buildings.[9] For the researcher the maps can be valuable because they show the proximity of townlands to each other, the location of churches where ancestors worshiped and met, the cross-roads where young people gathered to dance and court. The Index Maps are available from the Ordnance Survey headquarters in Dublin and Belfast.

The Ordnance Survey Memoirs

In the course of conducting the survey each officer was required by Colby to keep a journal of the scientific, economic and historical facts about the locality he was surveying. It was Colby's plan to publish this material to accompany the maps, since he reasoned that additional information was necessary to clarify place-names and other distinctive features of a parish. In 1833 Lieutenant Thomas Larcom, Colby's assistant in Dublin, enlarged the scope of the material to include all aspects of the country's life: population, religion, welfare, architecture, archaeology, politics and literature. Although journals had been written for all the counties of Ulster Province, an *Ordnance Survey Memoir*, the term used to describe these writings, was published only for the parish of Templemore in Co. Londonderry in 1837. The government would not support the continued expenditure of money and time on such a project and it was scrapped. Unpublished manuscripts, however, were deposited in the Royal Irish Academy in Dublin.[10] In 1990 the Institute of Irish Studies of The Queen's University of Belfast began publishing a small number of them. As of 1998 forty volumes of Ulster Province *Memoirs* have been published.[11] Published volumes are listed in Appendix No. 2.

For the family historian seeking a full understanding of the physical, historical and social background of an ancestor, the Memoirs are an essential source of information.

Parish of Drumloman, County Cavan
Statistical Memoir by Lieutenant Andrew Beatty, November 1835

GEOGRAPHY OR NATURAL STATE
Name
Drumloman is derived from 2 Irish words "drum" signifying "a back or ridge" and "lum" signifying "bare or lean. This derivation seems to be supported by the appearance and general character of the parish, the ground being hilly and the soil light and poor.

---

[9] Ibid, p. 46.
[10] J. H. Andrews, *History in the Ordnance Map: An introduction for the Irish readers* (Kerry: David Archer, 1993), p. 46.
[11] R. Dudley Edwards, "Preliminary Report On The Ordnance Survey Manuscripts," *Analecta Hibernia* 23 (1966) lists the Academy's holding for Antrim, Armagh, Cavan, Cork, Donegal, Down, Fermanagh, Galway, Leitrim, Londonderry, Longford, Louth, Mayo, Meath, Monaghan, Queens, Roscommon, Sligo, Tipperary, and Tyrone

MODERN TOPOGRAPHY OR ARTIFICIAL STATE
Villages
There are 3 small villages in the parish, namely Kilgolah, Kilcogy and Glen.
Kilgolah has fallen completely into decay. The houses are either in ruin or rapidly verging towards that state. There are not 20 houses in the village, all of them in the very poorest description and many of them propped up by pieces of timber to prevent their tumbling down, which gives the village a very desolate appearance. The ruin of an old barrack stands near the centre of the village.
The village of Kilcogy consists of 8 or 10 houses. There is a constabulary (barracks) in which a few police are stationed and a national school.
The village of Glen consists only of a public house and 3 or 4 huts. It is situated on the road from Granard to Ballynagh, in the southern part of the townland of Mullaghorne.

Public Buildings
The places of worship and the schoolhouses are the only public buildings the parish can boast of.
The church of the Established religion ... was built about 50 years ago and is a plain stone building without either a tower or spire. It is of the simplest structure and may defy the church's bitterest enemies to point out any ornament of which they cam complain. It will accommodate about 300 persons.
There are 3 Roman Catholic chapels, all of them very neat edifices, built of stone and within the last 10 years. They will accomodate each about 500 or 600 persons.

Manufactories and Mills
There are no manufactories in this parish. There are only 3 corn mills in operation, situated in the townlands of Drumbannew, Mullaghorne and Lower Megherboy.

ANCIENT TOPOGRAPHY
There are a great number of raths, doons or forts, as they are generally called in this part of the country, scattered throughout the country. None of these forts have been opened. Any attempt to do so would be looked on by the greater mass of the inhabitants of the parish as sacrilege. Only one or two of the forts have been laboured, the people, especially the Roman Catholic part of the population, fearing that some calamity would shortly happen to the person rash enough to attempt it, and they relate numerous instances of such calamities having happened.

SOCIAL ECONOMY
Schools
Schools have not long enough been established in the parish to enable us to see any improvement resulting from them. Their effect will be more plainly seen in the rising generation. The people are very anxious to have their children instructed and afford them every facility.

Poor
There is no provision for the poor, with the exception of the collections made at the different places of worship on the sabbath. They depend for subsistence on the charity of individuals.

Habits of People
The cottages are generally built of mud, only one-sixth being stone. They are thatched with small glass windows, 1-storey high, with only two rooms generally, sometimes 3, and seem to be lamentably devoid of comfort or cleanliness.
The food of the poorer classes consists chiefly of potatoes and buttermilk. In winter they are seldom able to get milk and they substitute a drink made of onions boiled in water. Some of them assert that they are in such poverty at times that they are unable to purchase salt. This seems almost incredible.

PRODUCTIVE ECONOMY
Weaving
Weaving coarse linens is practiced by the men in the summer time, when their farming does not occupy all their time. The women are employed in hand-spinning but of later years this has not given any fair remuneration for labour. The produce of the loom is consumed on the spot.

Holdings and Rent
The usual size of the holdings averages from 10 to 20 acres. These are generally held by leases of 1 life or 21 years or 3 lives or 31 years. The rent is paid wholly in money. The baneful practice of subletting is too much practiced in the parish. The holdings of the undertenants vary from 3 to 5 acres. The rent paid by them is paid partly by labour. The best land is let from 30s to 2 pounds, land of a middling quality from 20s to 30s and inferior land from 10s to 20s.
Tithes and county cess are the only taxes to which the tenants are liable.

Crops and Markets
The rotation of crops is generally potatoes and oats, or sometimes potatoes, wheat, oats.

The market towns are Granard, Ballynagh and Ballyheelan. Oats are bought up for exportation to England. They are carried to Drogheda, from whence they are shipped.

Figure 9. Transcribed from *Ordnance Survey Memoirs of Ireland*, Volume 40, Counties of South Ulster 1834-8, pp. 12-18. Institute of Irish Studies, The Queen's University of Belfast, Belfast, 1998.

THE FIRST VALUATION: THE TOWNLAND VALUATION ACT OF 1826

One year after the formation of the Boundary Office and the commencement of the Ordnance Survey, Parliament enacted 7 Geo. IV, Cap. 62 to provide a country-wide uniform system of property valuation in response to mounting antagonism with the current system for levying the county cess. However, it was not until 1830 that the agency and leadership to put the new legislation into operation was established. Five years after Richard Griffith had set up the Boundary Department, he undertook the additional responsibility of Commissioner of Valuation. He was directed by the Act to devise "a uniform Valuation of Lands and Tenements for the Purpose of the more equally levying of Grand Jury Rates and the County Cess Charges upon the Baronies, Parishes, and other Divisions" within each county[12]. Because the townland was the smallest land division generally recognized throughout the country by occupiers and governmental authorities, it was the unit by which land would be measured and valued. Richard Griffith's double responsibility as Chief Boundary Officer and as Commissioner of Valuation would occupy him for the next forty years of his career before the country-wide valuation was successfully completed in 1865.

Having completed the boundary demarcations of twelve counties, Griffith was confident that he could finish the remainder well in advance of the Royal Engineers surveyors who would follow in the wake of his perambulators. Griffith described in later years the procedure he used to employ the men to do the valuation under the Act of 1826.

> *"The Act required that they should be surveyors and valuators of land and houses. When I came to Co. Londonderry in 1830, I inquired of the proprietors, and their agents, who were the persons they employed to value for them before letting their lands, for it was a universal practice there (fortunately for me) to let lands by valuation, and not by tender [an amount of money offered by a tenant to rent a holding], as in other parts of Ireland. I then obtained the names of a number of professional surveyors and valuators who had been engaged ... ; and after a great deal of trouble, I fixed upon nine of them, and I collected them in the county of Londonderry; we began at Coleraine.*
>
> *"I read the Act of Parliament to them, and told them that the principle of valuation that I wished to follow was, "Live and let live," the principle on which ... the landlords in the north of Ireland let their lands ... and then we went to the land and dug up the soil. Each man formed his own opinion of the value of the land per acre. I wrote down my own bid first, then I obtained successively the bids of the nine valuers; I afterwards read them all out, and we all discussed the matter, and after some time came to a conclusion as to what was a fair price per acre. We went*

---

[12] 7 Geo. IV., Cap. 62, Section I.

through a number of fields ... and the next day I took them into another district,
where the soil was different, and went through the same process.
"This school was continued a month, and at the end of that time I separated them
into threes, putting one at the head of each party [a "baronial" valuator and his
two assistants], and went with each alternately for a week. After that I began the
valuation of the county of Londonderry." [13]

Beginning in the north of the island, Griffith's teams progressively worked their way south - county by county, townland by townland - a journey of seventeen years. He sent his first crew of three valuators in 1830 to Co.Londonderry where the mapping had been completed by Colby's Engineers.

For their guidance during these early field activities, Griffith found it necessary to frequently issue directives and instructions as questions arose among his staff or as he foresaw possible problems. He formalized these directives and instructions beginning in 1833 with the publication of the first of four manuals entitled *Instructions to the Valuators for the Uniform Valuation of Lands in Ireland* with other editions to follow in 1836, 1839, and 1852.[14]

The Machinery of the Townland Valuation

The Townland Valuation, as Griffith's first valuation was named, was primarily concerned with determining a nationwide uniform value of the soil and of the buildings erected on it as a tax basis. Identity of the persons responsible for the payment of taxes would eventually be the job of 'applotters' selected by the local Grand Jury to determine what proportion of the total county cess each occupier was to pay.[15] Under 7 Geo. IV. Cap. 62 and the amending legislation of 1831 and 1832 (1 & 2 Will. IV, Cap. 51 and 2 & 3 Will. IV, Cap. 73) two criteria were stipulated to determine the taxable value of a townland, one for land and one for houses. Land was to be valued at the rent a fair landlord could reasonably expect to receive based on its fertility calculated by a scale of prices listed in the legislation for wheat, oats, barley, potatoes, butter, beef, mutton and pork. This price structure was to be used throughout all counties so that the lands of Derry and Antrim, which were valued first, and those of Cork and Kerry, to be valued last, would thus be determined by a uniform scale. A house, on the other hand, was to be valued by the annual rent for which it would reasonably be let in the state in which it was found at the time of its valuation.

---

[13] Select Committee on General Valuation (Ireland), PP 1869 (362) IV, Question 1335
[14] Ibid. Question 2552.
[15] Tony McCarthy, *The Irish Roots Guide* (Dublin: The Lilliput Press, 1991), p. 41.

Valuation of Land

On setting out to begin their work each of the three teams of valuators was provided with the essential Ordnance Survey maps of the barony to which it was assigned, and each valuator was given a supply of printed sheets stitched together to form a 'field book' to record the details of the soil in each townland.

Two categories of land were subject to valuation, arable land (agricultural land, woods and 'plantations' of ornamental trees and bushes) and pasture land (grazing land for cattle and horses, 'bog' and 'turbary'). To determine a townland's fertility the team was directed to divide it into a number of 'lots' in "such a manner, that each portion, shall contain land of nearly the same quality and value."[16] Lines were drawn on the Ordnance Survey map to identify each lot by its soil quality. Arable land usually varied in lots of ten to thirty acres while bog and mountain land were not limited in size.

After numbering a lot and marking its lines on the map each valuator separately examined it by digging up its surface to determine the nature of the soil, its depth and the nature of the subsoil. Only by this procedure, not by the surface appearance of the soil, was the valuation to be determined stated Griffith "as a crop raised from poor shallow land highly manured might look better than a similar crop raised on good deep land badly cultivated, the object being that the quality of the ground, and not the actual state of cultivation is the criterion on which the valuation is to be made."[17] By analyzing the kind and quality of soil (arable, stony, sandy, grassy, wet, etc.) a valuator would individually estimate the amount of wheat, for example, that the given lot could produce and set a value by the acre for such soil. By way of illustration, an acre of good soil that might produce three hundred weight of wheat was to be valued "at the general average price of ten shillings per hundred weight" as specified by the Act.[18] Without any communication with his colleagues he entered this figure for the lot in his field book.[19] After the members of the team had determined their independent valuation of the lot, the baronial valuator recorded his and his assistants' figures in his field book. When a consensus of value was agreed upon by the team, it was entered into the baronial valuator's book. Ultimately three separate field books were produced for each parish by the team.

When testifying before the Select Committee on County Cess, Griffith was asked whether the "boundary of a townland is the boundary of a parish, are the boundaries in any degree commensurate?" He responded:

> *"The boundaries of parishes are always boundaries of townlands; that is to say,*

---

[16] Richard Griffith, *Instructions to the Valuators and Surveyors appointed under the 15th & 16th Vict. c. 63, for the Uniform Valuation of Lands and Tenements in Ireland*, Section 25.
[17] *Minutes of Evidence Taken Before Select Committee on County Cess (Ireland) 1836*, Question 595.
[18] Griffith, *Instructions*, Op cit., Section 18.
[19] "Field", as used in this context, refers to the details of soil composition and productivity.

one townland cannot be contained in two parishes; it sometimes happens that an estate may lie on both sides of the boundary of a parish, and that the townland in each parish is called by the same name, and is considered to be one townland, but in such cases I have always divided the townland, and added the word upper or lower, east or west, to the original name, to serve to distinguish them. As each parish will be separately assessed, it is necessary that no confusion should arise as to the boundaries of any denomination or division belonging to it, consequently in all cases the boundary of a parish must likewise be the boundary of a townland as far as that parish or the county assessment is concerned."[20]

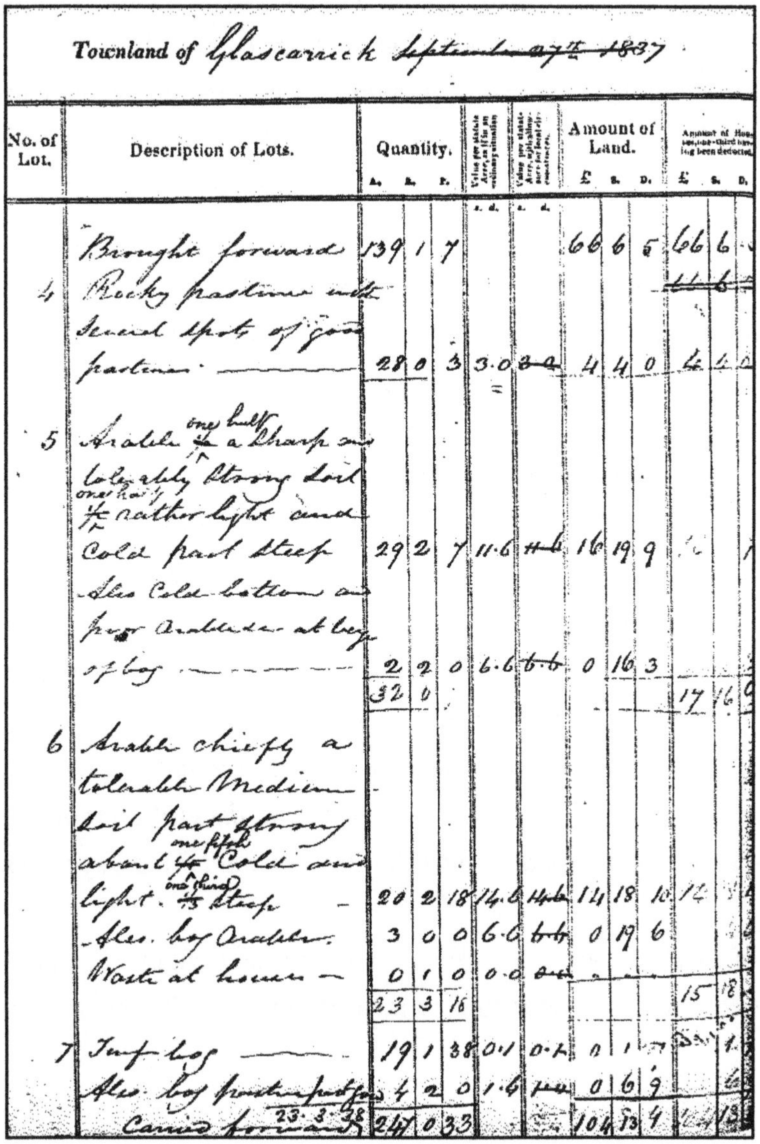

Figure 10. Field Book, Townland of Glasscarrick, Co. Cavan, 1837.
Valuation Office

---

[20] *Minutes on County Cess (Ireland) 1836, Op. cit.,* Question 690.

Valuation of Houses

The Townland Act of 1826 (7 Geo. IV, Cap. 62), Section VII, required that   *"... all Houses shall be valued at the Sum or Rent for which each such House respectively could be let by the Year ...."* However, in October 1831, sixteen months after the 1830 commencement of the valuation process in Co. Londonderry, the Act was amended to read *" ... whereas it is not expedient or necessary ... to include in the Valuation ... Houses of a perishable Nature and inconsiderate Value, ... That no House for which a greater Sum or Rent by the Year than Three Pounds could not be obtained ... shall be included in the Valuation ...* [21] This amendment, in effect, exempts occupiers of such houses from this portion of the cess. Ten months later in August 1832 the Act was further amended *"That all Houses ... except] Houses of an annual Rent ... not exceeding Three Pounds ... shall be valued, and ... entered in the Field Books* .[22] In August 1836 at the suggestion of the Commissioner of Valuation the £3 house exemption was increased by Parliament to £5 and remained so until 1846.[23] And finally the *Instructions Book 1833* fixed that *"... to determine the value of any house [with its outbuildings, barns, stables warehouses, offices], the Baronial Valuator, and his Assistants, are ... to ascertain by measurement of the exterior walls, the number of measures, each consisting of ten square feet, it contains.*[24]

To determine the required dimensions one of the Assistant Valuators accompanied by a laborer measured each house in the townland and recorded the data in a "house book," the second set of printed sheets provided by the Valuation Office. He was to measure the length and width of the building to calculate the number of "ten square feet" measures, and then to measure its height. The occupier's name accompanied the noted measurements. In the house book of Roshin townland in Co. Donegal, as an example, Henry Wm. Hayward's first structure is 17.0 feet in length and 21.0 feet in breadth, a total of 357.0 square feet or 35.7 measures, and it is 13.6 feet in height. After the Assistant entered the measurements of all houses in his copy, he prepared two additional copies, one each for the Baronial Valuator and second Assistant.

Supplied with their house books, each valuator *"having examined the building with care ... is to enter in his book ... the quality letter... which according to the tables [shown below], determines the price at which each measure containing ten square feet, multiplied by the height is to be calculated ... ."*[25]

Houses were of three classes: new, medium and old; and within each class a house was assigned a *quality letter*[26] that best described its state of repair, age and construction:

---

[21] 1 & 2 Wm. IV., Cap. 51, Section I.
[22] 2 & 3 Will., Cap. 73, Section II.
[23] 6 & 7 Wm. IV, Cap. 84, Section X.
[24] Griffith, *Instructions*, Op. cit., Section 147.
[25] Ibid, Section 151.
[26] Ibid, Section 148.

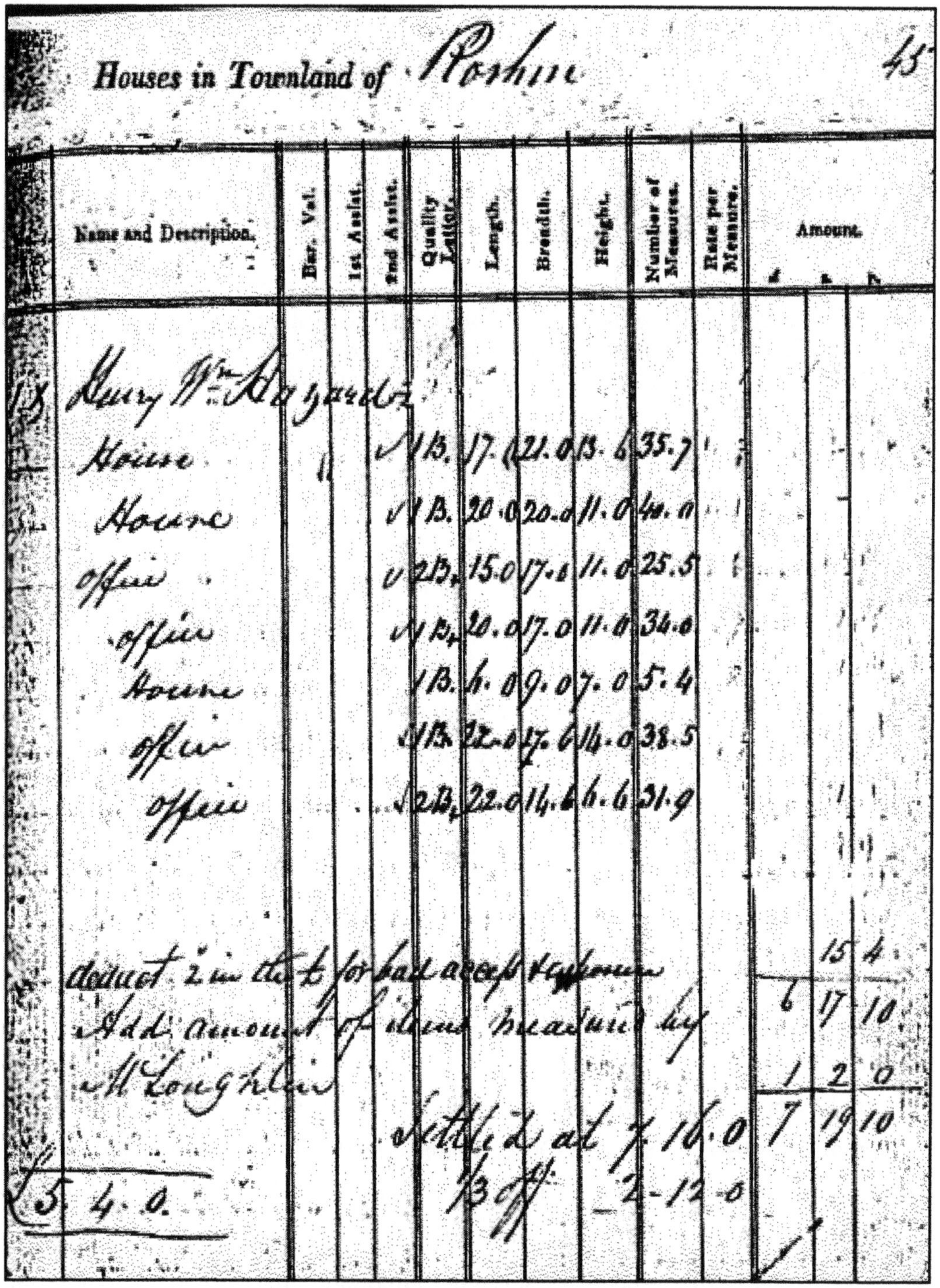

Figure 11. House Book, Townland of Roshin, Co. Donegal.
Valuation Office

New or Nearly New
A+ *Built or ornamented with cut stone, and of superior solidity, and finish.*
A *Very substantial building, and finish, without cut stone ornament*
A- *Ordinary building and finish or either of the above when built 20 or 25 years.*

<u>Medium</u>

B+   *Medium (not new,) but in sound order, and good repair;*
B   *Medium, slightly decayed, but in good repair:*
B-   *Medium, deteriorated by age, and not in perfect repair.*

<u>Old</u>

C+   *Old, but in repair:*
C   *Old and out of repair:*
C-   *Old, and dilapidated, scarcely habitable*

Each letter was further qualified with the number 1, 2 or 3:
1   *Slated roof house of stone or brick with lime mortar*
2   *Thatched roof house of stone or brick with lime mortar*
3   *Thatched house of stone walls with mud mortar or mud walls of the best kind*
4   *Basement stories of slated houses used as dwellings*[27]

The baronial valuator followed a procedure similar to the one he used to record his assistants' soil assessments. After entering a quality letter and number in his book, the baronial valuator copied the quality letters set by his assistants. Reading read aloud all three opinions the baronial valuator invited discussion to arrive at a quality letter acceptable to all three of them which was then entered in their house books.

Upon completion of the lot descriptions and house measurements for the civil parish, the final procedure for the team was to prepare a 'fair copy' of the field book.[28] Other than the required data, all calculations, notations and the like were to be omitted from the clean copy. An alphabetical index of the townlands was to be added, and the names of occupiers of houses valued at or above the £3 or £5 exemption in each townland were to be copied from the house books and entered in the field book. Together with the original three field and three house books as well as the amended OS maps, the fair copy was sent or taken to Dublin where the valuators and office staff made final calculations, arranged data, and ultimately prepared selected information for publication, as required by the Act, in the *Dublin Gazette* newspaper. This printed version of the Townland Valuation is simply a statistical summary of land and building values with no occupier names included.

During the mid-1940s the Valuation Office bound together in a hard-covered volume a field book and its accompanying house book, if there was one, of the Townland Valuation for each civil parish in the Republic of Ireland. These volumes, called "townland valuation field books," are accessible at the Valuation Office. Additional surviving unbound copies for the Republic are at the National Archives of Ireland, and those for Northern Ireland are at Belfast's PRONI.

---

[27] Ibid, Sectkion 158.
[28] Ibid, Section 36.

PRINTED at the OFFICE of the GENERAL ADVERTISER, DUBLIN, OCTOBER 2, 1847

GENERAL VALUATION OF IRELAND—COUNTY OF CLARE

COUNTY OF CLARE.

VALUATION OF LANDS, &c,

WITHIN THE SEVERAL PARISHES AND TOWNLANDS IN THE SAID COUNTY,

MADE IN PURSUANCE OF

THE ACT 6 and 7 WILLIAM IV, CAP 84,

FOR THE

UNIFORM VALUATION OF LANDS IN IRELAND.

BARONY OF BUNRATTY LOWER

Parishes and Townlands		Quantity			Annual Value of Land			Annual Value of Houses, deducting one-third			Total		
		A	R	P	£	s	d	£	s	d	£	s	d
BUNRATTY													
Bunratty East	...	394	2	0	447	14	0	46	3	0	493	17	0
Bunratty West	...	416	0	29	306 577/10	16	0	18	13	0	596	9	0
Clonmoney North	...	359	2	5	342	11	0	3	18	0	346	9	0
Clonmoney South	...	391	0	14	554	6	0	—			554	6	0
Clonmoney West	...	737	1	19	928	13	0	22	0	0	950	13	0
Cloverhill ...	...	52	3	26	37	19	0	3	16	0	41	15	0
Corlack ...	...	108	0	35	77	1	0	9	4	0	86	5	0
Deerpark ...	...	65	1	26	46	0	0	—			46	0	0
Islands in the River Shannon :													
Saints Island	...	13	3	6	16	11	0	—			16	11	0
Sod Island	...	0	1	26	0	5	0	—			0	5	0
Little Quay Island	...	0	3	17	0	10	0	—			0	10	0
Small Island of no agricultural value		0	0	13	—			—					
Quay Island	...	22	0	18	25	13	0	—			25	13	0
Woodpark ...	...	184	1	13	118	15	0	12	0	0	130	15	0
Total		2746	3	7	3178 14 0 3137. 13. 0			115	14	0	3269 8 0 3253. 7. 0		
EXEMPTIONS													
Bunratty East, Police Barrack	...	—			—			18	16	0	18	16	0
Bunratty West, Grave-yard	...	0	2	10	0	9	0	—			0	9	0
Clonmoney West, Roman Catholic Chapel and Yard	...	0	0	15	—			7	17	0	7	17	0
— National School-house and Yard	...	0	0	20	—			8	10	0	8	10	0
Total of Exemptions		0	3	5	0	9	0	35	3	0	35	12	0
CLONLOGHAN													
Ballinooskny	...	190	2	39	177	0	0	13	10	0	190	10	0
Ballymurtagh	...	77	3	17	72	0	0	16	12	0	88	12	0
Caherteige ...	...	400	1	7	389	0	0	—			389	0	0
Clonloghan	...	401	1	6	285	3	0	4	14	0	289	17	0
Drumgeely	...	216	0	16	249	7	0	4	5	0	253	12	0
Islands :—Asscarrick	...	0	0	33	—			—					
Killulla ...	...	380	1	32	280	16	0	3	10	0	284	6	0
Knocksun ...	...	121	2	8	116	5	0	6	6	0	122	11	0
Leamaneighbeg	...	95	2	3	47	4	0	—			47	4	0
Leamaneighmore	...	215	1	9	156	5	0	16	3	0	172	8	0
Lisconor ...	...	102	3	17	70	17	0	—			70	17	0
Lislea ...	...	133	3	39	71	4	0	—			71	4	0
Lismacleane	...	100	3	31	152	0	0				152	0	0

Figure 12. Townland Valuation, County of Clare, 1847,
as published by the GENERAL ADVERTISER DUBLIN.
National Library of Ireland

It has been said that no record was kept of structures in the Townland Valuation judged to be less than £3 or £5 in value. Such was not Griffith's practice as is evidenced by his statement before the Cess Committee, *"I consider myself bound by the Valuation Act to value every thing, and afterwards to exempt such portion of land, or such houses as are legally exempt."*[29] In light of his expression, the statement in the field book found at the foot of each townland, *There are no houses in this townland worth £3 (or £5) a year,* should not deter researchers from searching for an ancestor in the accompanying house book. As shown in the house book for the townland of Ballycorey, Co. Clare (figure 13) there are houses valued considerably lower than the £5 cut-off; for example, John McMahon's dwelling houses are valued at 3s/3d and 13s/6d. As required by the Act these houses were "exempt" from the final calculations made in the Valuation Office before setting the townland's assessment.

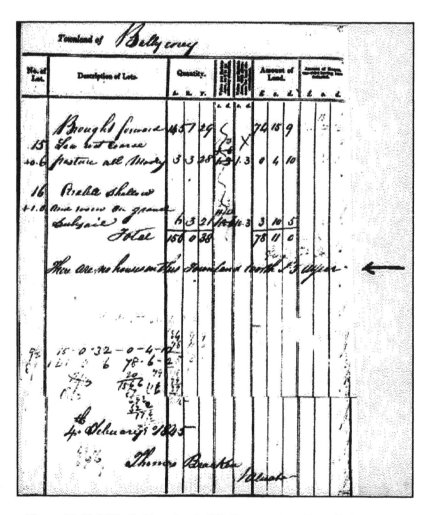

Figure 13. Field Book, Townland of Ballycorey, Co. Clare. Valued 1845.
Note the arrow indicating that *There are no houses in this townland worth £5 a year.*
Valuation Office

---

[29]*Minutes on County Cess (Ireland) 1836, Op. cit.,* Question No. 652.

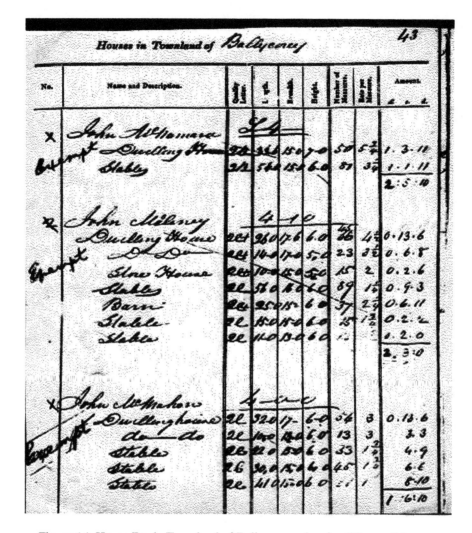

Figure 14. House Book, Townland of Ballycorey, showing "Exempt" houses.
Valuation Office

A relatively unknown source of occupier names is the townland field book itself. Valuators sometimes identified the occupier of a "lot" by name for no discernible reason as is seen in figure 15.

In another example, the townland of Closutton in the parish of Killinane, Co. Carlow was valued in 1841; its field book names only two occupiers of houses worth £5 or more. However, the field book's lot descriptions identify by name no less than twenty-five individuals as holders of the various "lots" within the townland[30].

Although accessible only in Ireland, the field and house books of the Townland Valuation should be searched to identity an ancestor in a time period often lacking church records and census documents.

---

[30] Valuation Office, *Field book of the Parish of Killinane, Barony of Idrone West, Co. Carlow*, pp.4-8, 21-22

Field books presently available in the Valuation Office that contain occupier names in their lot descriptions are listed in Appendix No. 3.

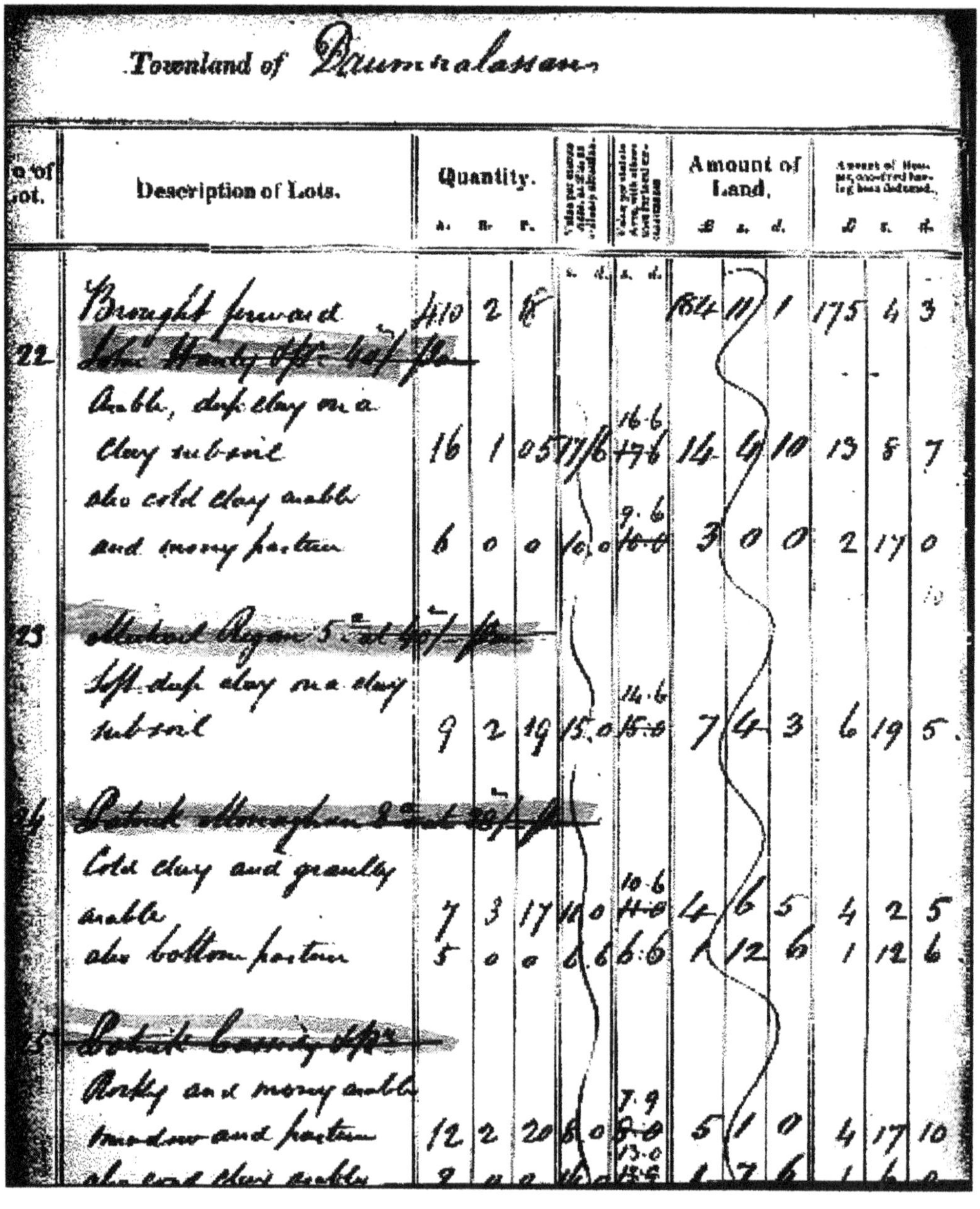

Figure 15. Field Book, Townland of Drumnalassan, Co. Mayo. Dated 1840
Valuation Office

The Poor Law Act of 1838

During the years the Townland Valuation was being conducted an alarming increase in the number of people in Ireland unable to support themselves was evident to civil authorities and religious leaders. Although relief for the poor and destitute of England was being provided by the government, no such system existed for Ireland. What assistance there was came from private and church charitable organizations at home and abroad. While the local Irish grand jury supported a number of activities with its county cess, it did not provide specifically for the relief of its poor and destitute, nor did the Townland Valuation make any such provision.

Consequently, Parliament legislated in 1838 "An Act for the more effectual Relief of the destitute Poor in Ireland."[31] The Act declared that relief was to be provided within a workhouse system.[32] The funds needed to construct and support the workhouses were to be raised by taxing "... *the person in actual Occupation of the Rateable Property at the time of the Rate [being] made ...,"* be he a renter, a lease holder or an owner, on the value of his 'tenement.'[33] The legislation called for the country to be divided into administrative districts known as Poor Law Unions, each to be a geographical joining of townlands within ten miles of a large market town in which the workhouse was to be located.[34] Accessible by the main roads of the area, the journey to the workhouse was less difficult for the sick and infirm, the children, and the physically weakened pauper. Boundaries of unions often crossed county, barony and civil parish lines; they did not, however, intersect townland boundaries.

Acting independently of the local Grand Jury and its on-going Townland Valuation under the supervision of Richard Griffith, the governing body of each union, a Board of Guardians, was permitted to use existing local surveys of tenements and their valuations to determine its poor rates. However, Boards were permitted to initiate new surveys if they were dissatisfied with their current valuations. Many unions took the opportunity to employ local surveyors and land valuators to prepare a new base for setting their rates. The Poor Law Act required a book to be kept containing the particulars of the valuation listing among other information the *name of the occupier* of the tenement, the *name of the owner*, a *description of the property* and its *location within the union*.[35] Unfortunately, the Rate Books, as they are called, survive for only six unions for the years 1842-1855.[36] Downpatrick Union in Co. Down, Newry Union partly in Counties Down and Armagh, and Clogher Union partly in Counties Monaghan and Tyrone are accesible at PRONI. Kilmallock Union partly in Counties Limerick and Cork is at the Limerick Regional Archives in Limerick City. Nenagh and Thurles Unions, both in Co. Tipperary, are in the Tipperary County Library at Thurles. Rate books of the Nenagh and Thurles Unions have been microfilmed by the Genealogical Society of Utah and are available in the Family History Library, Salt Lake City, and its world-wide Family History Centers.[37]

---

[31] 1 & 2 Vict., Cap, 56.
[32] John O'Connor, *The Workhouses of Ireland*   (Dublin: Anvil Books, 1995].
[33] 1 & 2 Vict.,Op. cit., Section LXXI.
[34] Idem, Section XV.
[35] Idem, Section LXV.
[36] Deidre Lindsay and David Fitzpatrick, *Records of the Irish Famine* (Dublin: Irish Famine Network, 1993).
[37] Family History Library film numbers: Thurles Union # 1279316, item 8; Nenagh Union #1279315, items 1 - 4.

By mid-1841 there were 130 Poor Law Unions formed, and within two years over 100 work-houses were in operation. Due to the density of the pauper population in thirty-two unions, their number between 1848 and 1850 was increased to 163 by subdividing some of the larger unions. Rates among the unions varied greatly depending upon the pauper population being provided for in their local workhouses.

Because the poor rate valuation system was to be carried out locally by a Board of Guardians of the Poor elected by the rate-payers, each union was subdivided into electoral divisions. Each electoral division comprised a number of adjoining townlands whose total population averaged 4000 persons[38]; its purpose was to choose representatives of its rate payers to serve on the Board of Guardians.[39] The Act also provided for taxing each electoral division for its share of the general ex-penses of the union, for the cost incurred for the relief of paupers identified in the workhouse's register as being its residents; paupers not identified as residents of a particular electoral division were to be charged to the union at large.[40]

With the inauguration of the poor rate valuation for the country, there were now two local tax-ing systems in operation, the county cess and the poor rate. This double tax burden created consid-erable unrest among the ratepayers. Particularly aroused were critics of the Poor Law rate system who claimed that persons employed to value property were often local farmers unskilled in valuing or were friends and associates of large landholders whose holdings they undervalued. The opera-tion of the electoral divisions was a further source of discord:

> "... although arranged with the utmost care ... the electoral divisions did not work
> smoothly. Their separate chargeability interfered with the efficient action of the
> unions for general purposes, as in the case of emigration, and led to struggles and
> contention in the board of guardians as soon as the unions got finally into opera-
> tion, each union endeavoring to relieve itself from the charge of a registered pau-
> per, by fixing it upon some other, or by casting it upon the union at large ... ."[41]

Moreover, the Boards of Guardians were experiencing great difficulty in collecting rates from people who themselves were on the borderline of destitution.[42] Boards lobbied the authorities in Dublin to amend the Poor Law Act to make the landlord of a tenement at or under £5 in value solely liable for the rates.[43] The request was partially granted in 1843 making landlords of holdings valued at or below £4 fully liable for the payment of the rates. However, the amendment was to cause fu-

---

[38] Nichols, Op. cit. , p.304.
[39] 1 & 2 Vict., Cap. 56, Section XVIII.
[40] Ibid, Section XLIV.
[41] Nichols, Op. cit., p. 288.
[42] Helen Burke, *The People and The Poor Law in 19th Century Ireland*, (West Sussex, England: Argus Press, 1987), pp. 80-81.
[43] *18th Annual Report of the English Commissioners*, (London: 1842), p. 39.

ture problems because it gave landlords added incentive to evict tenants and avoid paying the tax on their holdings.

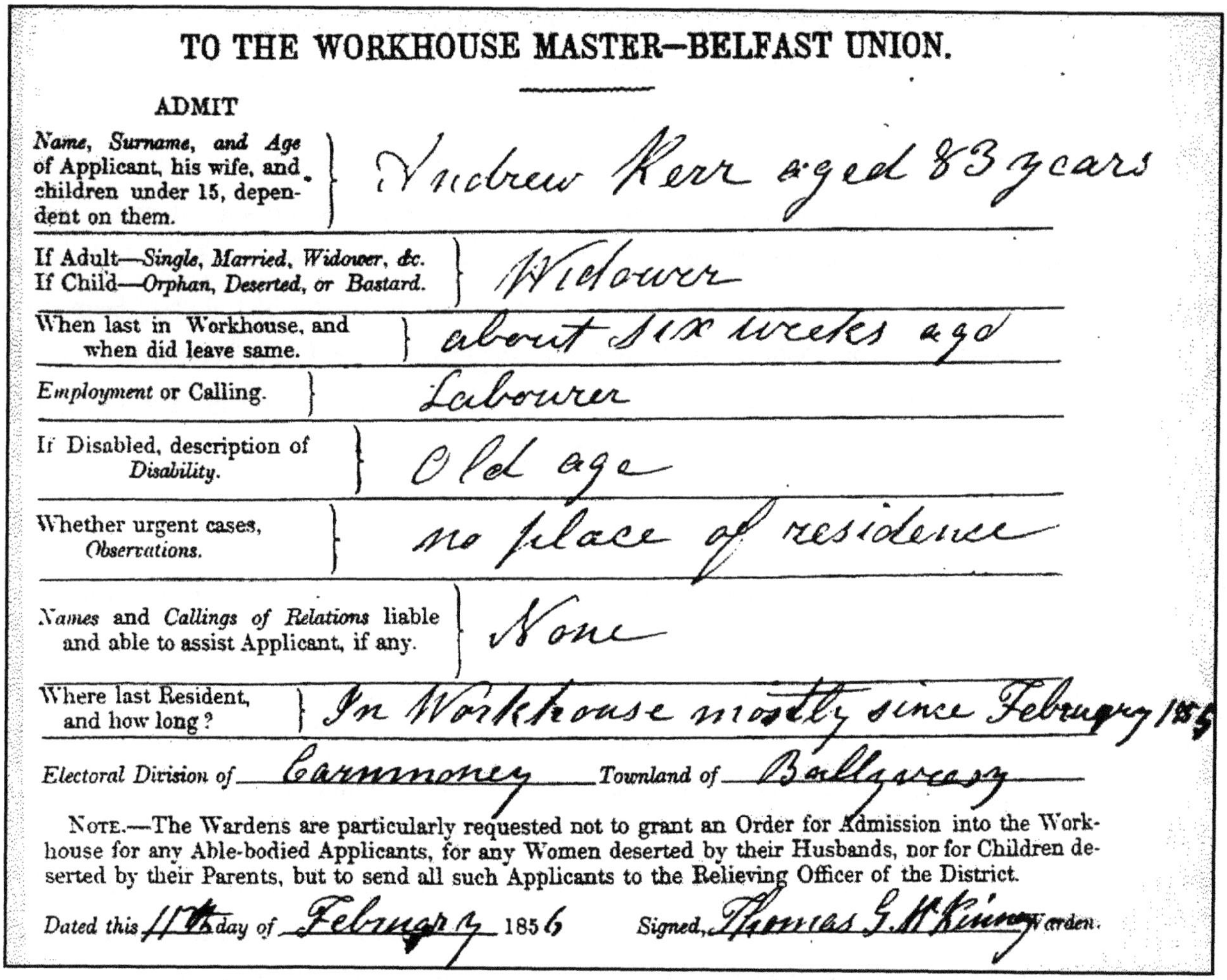

TO THE WORKHOUSE MASTER—BELFAST UNION.

ADMIT

Name, Surname, and Age of Applicant, his wife, and children under 15, dependent on them.	Andrew Kerr aged 83 years
If Adult—Single, Married, Widower, &c. If Child—Orphan, Deserted, or Bastard.	Widower
When last in Workhouse, and when did leave same.	about six weeks ago
Employment or Calling.	Labourer
If Disabled, description of Disability.	Old age
Whether urgent cases, Observations.	no place of residence
Names and Callings of Relations liable and able to assist Applicant, if any.	None
Where last Resident, and how long?	In Workhouse mostly since February 185

Electoral Division of __Carnmoney__   Townland of __Ballyvrean__

NOTE.—The Wardens are particularly requested not to grant an Order for Admission into the Workhouse for any Able-bodied Applicants, for any Women deserted by their Husbands, nor for Children deserted by their Parents, but to send all such Applicants to the Relieving Officer of the District.

Dated this _11th_ day of _February_ 1856   Signed, _Thomas G. M'Kinney_ Warden.

Figure 16. Admission Ticket to the Belfast Union Workhouse signed by the Workhouse Warden

The Townland Valuation: Parliament Reexamines

Because the Townland Valuation gave only a description of the lots into which the land had been divided for valuing and did not generally identify their occupiers, rate payers had begun to question the accuracy of their tax assessments.[44] As early as 1836 Griffith was asked if there was "*a mode by which an individual land holder can ascertain how far he has been correctly valued [in the Townland Valuation] in comparison wthi his neighbors.*" He responded that "*... a rate payer cannot without difficulty ascertain the value put on his portion of it.*"[45]

In December 1843 while testifying before the Devon Commission members who were investigating the Townland Valuation because of increasing complaints from landlords and tenants, clergy and influential landowners, Richard Griffith was asked if his valuation system could also be used to determine the "*poor law rate or any other [rate],*" and he responded that it had already been used by Poor Law Unions in several counties and "*the result has given general satisfaction.*"[46]

As a result of Griffith's testimony and the mounting dissatisfaction with the cess valuations, the Devon Commission recommended to Parliament that the townland valuation be discontinued and "*... that a tenement valuation applicable to the imposition and levy of all local taxes be substituted.*" The Commission further "*... suggests that the county cess and the poor rate should be levied together, and that the same principle of payment between landlord and tenant be applied to both taxes.*"[47]

Although Parliament did not immediately follow the Committee's recommendation, the Lord Lieutenant of Ireland, under authority granted to him by the Act of 1826, Section VIII, directed Griffith in anticipation of subsequent Parliamentary legislation to change the county cess base of taxation from "townland" to "tenement," the base currently being used by the Poor Law Unions in their rate system. The Lord Lieutenant accordingly issued on 26 October 1844 a document titled "Instructions relative to a new system to be adopted by the Commissioner of Valuation in making out the Field Books and Valuation Maps, under the 6 & 7 Wm. IV., Cap. 84, pursuant to the 8th section of that Act."

"*In carrying the [Townland] Valuation Act into effect, His Excellency finds from the printed book of instructions [published in 1839]... that the boundaries of each of the lots shall coincide, as far as possible with the boundaries of farms... he directs that in future the following system shall be adopted:*

> *1. That every tenement, no matter how minute, shall be entered separately in the field book, and have a distinguishing number prefixed to it, and that the Christian*

---

[44] Minutes on County Cess, Op. cit., Question 673.

[45] Ibid, Question 675.

[46] British Parlimentary Papers, "Minutes of Evidence Taken Before Select Committee To Inquire Into The Occupation of Land In Ireland, HC 1845 (606) I, Questions 48-51.

[47] British Parlimentary Papers, Report to the Queen's Most Excellent Majesty, HC 1845 (605), Vol. XIX, page 11.

*name and surname of the occupant shall be inserted opposite to such number, to-
gether with a description of the soil, and the content and value of the tenement.*

*2. Where tenants hold in 'rundale' or in common ... the name of every occupant
should be written in the field book, and annexed to his name the proportion or
fraction of the whole, that he holds.*

*3. That the value of every house ... shall be entered in the field book as part of the
value of the tenement; but where the house ... shall not amount to the sum of £5 in
annual value, the amount of such building shall be entered in a column for exemp-
tions, and shall not be included in the amount of the value of the tenement.*[48]

At the time the Lord Lieutenant's directive was issued, all counties of Ulster Province had been
completed under the Townland Valuation Act and published in the *Dublin Gazette*. In the Province
of Leinster seven of the eleven counties were completed, and in Connaught only Galway remained
(Appendix No. 5). With the exception of Co. Clare in Munster Province which was already under-
way, the remaining counties of Cork, Kerry, Limerick, Tipperary, and Waterford were now to be
valued under the new "Instructions" issued by the Lord Lieutenant. And because serious errors in
its original Ordnance Survey maps had raised questions about the accuracy of its valuation, the
County of Dublin was to be revalued.

Testifying before the Devon Commission two months after the issuance of the Lord Lieutenant's directive, Griffith indicated that he had already begun using a *tenement* valuation to levy the
county cess in Co. Tipperary and in Co. Dublin. Examination of the Townland Valuation field
books in the Valuation Office for Cork, Dublin, Kerry, Limerick, Tipperary and Waterford will
show occupier names appended to the "lot description" of the holdings conforming to the Lord
Lieutenant's *Instructions* of October 1844 (Appendix No. 3)

Aware of increasing concern among members of Parliament and their constituents because of
the growing expense of the on-going valuation, Griffith undertook to modify the composition of the
field team for the "tenement" valuation by substituting a single valuator and a surveyor in place of
a baronial valuator with two assistants. He eliminated the practice of a 'check valuation' of an entire
townland and adopted a procedure which he claimed was " *cheaper ... and a great deal more accurate.* "[49] Under his new system a single check valuator examined only sample sections of tenements
and townlands to verify the accuracy of the original valuation rather than inspecting an entire townland.

---

[48] *Additional Instructions to the Valuators Employed under 6 & 7 Wm. IV, Cap. 84* (Dublin: Alexander Thom,
1844), p.3. The minimum exemption of a £5 valuation would be eliminated in future legislation.
[49] Select Committee on General Valuation (Ireland), HC 1869 (362) IV, Question 1490.

THE SECOND VALUATION: THE TENEMENT VALUATION ACT OF 1846

Enacting 9 & 10 Vict., Cap. 110 on 28 August 1846 Parliament put into effect recommendations of the Devon Commission. The Act was drafted to conclude the country-wide cess valuation in the remaining counties of Munster Province (Cork, Kerry, Limerick, Tipperary, and Waterford) and to revalue Co. Dublin. Its second objective was to demonstrate within the six counties the impartiality of Griffith's valuing scheme as a base for an evenhanded poor rate system and to guage its acceptability among the Guardians and rate-payers.

The Act required the Valuation Office staff to collect specific valuation details to enable grand juries and Poor Law Guardians to set their tax rates. The structure of the valuations was to be by barony within a county, then by civil parish, townland and tenement within the barony. Some data would be common to both assessments, that is, the name of a tenement's occupier and of his/her landlord; the holding's size, and the dimensions of each building on it. Additional data would be unique to the requirements of the county cess or the poor rates.

When informed by the Valuation Office of the total taxable value of land and buildings within a barony, the grand jury set the tax rate necessary to raise the money required for its activities. The 'applotment' subsequently imposed upon a tenement was paid by its occupier.[50] Likewise the Board of Guardians also fixed its poor rates on the taxable value of holdings within its boundaries, but its taxes were collected half from the occupier of a holding and half from its landlord.[51]

To obtain information needed by the valuator to begin his work in the field, a Valuation Office surveyor was sent to perambulate each townland within a barony's civil parishes. He carried a notebook and the maps (6 inches to a mile) drawn several years earlier by the Ordnance Survey team showing townland boundaries to accomplish the activities described in Griffith's "Instructions for Land Surveyors:"[52]

> *1. In the barony entrusted to his charge, the surveyor is to go over the whole of every townland, and to mark the boundary of every tenement on the map with a dotted or fine red line; putting a number on the map on each tenement, and a corresponding number in his field book, with the name and surname of each occupant annexed.*
>
> *2. In towns, or the neighbourhood of towns, where the tenements are so small, say less than one acre, that there would not be room on the map to write a number on each, the surveyor is to use his judgment in uniting several of them, say from five to twenty of them in one division or lot with a dotted line and insert a number within the lot. It will then be necessary to arrange these small tenements consecutively ...*

---

[50] 9 & 10 Vict., Cap. 110, Section XXXIV.
[51] Select Committee, HC 1869 (362) IV, Op. cit., Question 4197.
[52] *Instructions 1844, Op. cit.*

and to number them in his field book 1, 2, 3, 4 &c. writing the Christian name and surname of the occupant opposite each number."

3. The Surveyor ... is to measure all houses and offices and to attach to each in his field book the quality letter ... ."

During the plotting of a tenement, the surveyor asked the occupant or the landlord, "What is the rent?" and "How is the tenement held [by lease, by the year, owned]?"[53] and entered these details as well in his notebook. Those occupants he was unable to question would be sought later by the valuator.

Completing the perambulation of a district, the surveyor returned to Dublin where his maps and notebook were used to produce a series of additional books needed by the staff to finish the valuation process. The surveyor's notebook was dubbed a "perambulation" book to distinguish it from similar books used to collect data during the earlier townland valuations.

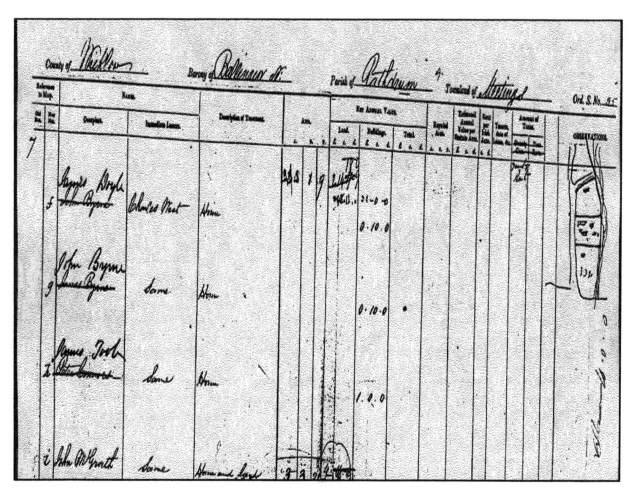

Figure 17. Perambulation Book, Townland of Meetings, Parish of Rathdrum, Co. Wicklow.
Valuation Office

---

[53] Select Committee on General Valuation (Ireland), HC 1869 (362) IV, Question 2012.

Three formats of column headings of the perambulation book have been seen in the Valuation Office and in the National Archives of Ireland. Basically they contain the same data to be gathered by the surveyors and valuators, although there are a few significant pieces of information not found in all three formats. For example, only Form 3 shows the amount of taxes paid to the county cess and the poor rate.

FORM 1	FORM 2	FORM 3
County	County	County
Barony	Barony	Barony
Parish	Parish	Parish
Townland	Townland	Townland
	Ord. S No.	Ord.S. No.

No. and Letters on Field Sheet	Reference to Map
	    Original
	    Revised
		Reference to Map

Names
    Occupiers
    Immediate Lessors
	Names
	    Occupiers
	    Immediate Lessors
		Names
		    Occupiers
		    Immediate Lessors

Description of Tenement	Description of Tenements
	    Soil
		Description of Tenements
		    Soil

Area (Acres Roods Perches)	Area (A R P)	Area (A R P)

- - - - - -	Value per Statute Acre
	    As if in ordinary situation.
	    With allowance for local
	    circumstances.
		Value per Statute Acre
		    As if in ordinary situation.
		    With allowance for local
		    circumstances.

Net Annual Value
    Land (£ -s-d)
    Buildings (£-s-d)
    Total   (£p-s-d)
	Net Annual Value
	    Land (£-s-d)
	    Buildings (£-s-d)
	    Total (£-s-d)
		Net Annual Value
		    Land (£-s-d)
		    Buildings (£-s-d)
		    Total (£-s-d)

Tenure, date of Lease, &c.	Total Rent, Tenure, and Date of Lease or Take	Tenure, Date of Lease, &c Reputed Area (A R P)
- - - - -	Estimated Net Annual Value of Tenement	Estimated Annual Value per Statute Acre
Rent per Irish Acre (s. d.)	Rent per Irish Acre	Rent per Irish Acre
Total Rent (£. s. d.)	(See Tenure, above)	. - - - - - -
English Acres Reduced to Irish (A. R. P.) Irish Acres (A. R. P.)	Reputed Area of Tenement	(See Tenure, above.)

- - - - -		Amount of Taxes
		    County Cess
		    Poor Rate

OBSERVATIONS Surveyor's opinion of Land per Statute Acre	- - - - - OBSERVATIONS	OBSERVATIONS

Figure 18. Perambulation Book Formats
Valuation Office

The Valuation Documents of the 1846 Act

The "Perambulation Book," as compiled by the surveyor and the valuator in the field, was the database used by the staff of the Valuation Office to generate the details required by the Act for publication to the Board of Guardians and the grand jury to set their tax rates. The researcher should be aware that some of the Perambulation Books for the six counties were transferred in the 1940s from the Valuation Office to the National Archives of Ireland where they were mistakenly catalogued as "Tenure Books." A catalogue of these books labeled "V.O.6 Record of Tenure Books 1841-1851" will be found on the open shelves of the Archives Reading Room; a few perambulation books are also listed in the Miscellaneous Books section of the "House Books Finding Aid" in the Reading Room.

A "House Book" lists the quality letter and dimensions of each tenement's buildings (house, barn, stable, piggery, etc.) with the occupier's name. All structures were taxed regardless of their value, the £5 restriction on buildings having been repealed by the 1846 Act. The House Books for the six counties are accessible at the National Archives and are catalogued in a binder on the open shelves entitled "Valuation Office - House Books."

"Quarto Books" are the house books for large towns showing the rent paid by year or by lease, the value of the house, and the name of the occupier; the landlord is not named. The extant twelve Quarto Books are available at the National Archives, Dublin.

A "Rent Book," arranged by the landlord's name for each of his tenements in a townland, was assembled by the Office staff from the information in the Perambulation Book to compare a holding's rent with the assessed value assigned by the valuator. A diverse and incomplete collection of Rent Books is available at the National Archives (Carlow, Clare, Cork, Dublin, Kerry, Kildare, Kilkenny, Leix, Limerick, Mayo, Offaly, Tipperary, Waterford and Wicklow). An inventory of the Rent Books by barony is included in the "Valuation Office - House Books" finding aid binder noted above.

The original "Maps" used in conjunction with the Poor Rate Perambulation Books are no longer at the Valuation Office; they are stored in the National Archives where they are not yet available for researchers.

The Poor Rate Valuation in the 1846 Act

In Ringroe townland, parish of Ballyfoyle, Co. Cork, both Julia Coughlin with her house and no land and her neighbor Luke J. Shea, Esq. holding 119 acres were to be valued for payment of poor rate taxes regardless of the size of their holdings.[54] The taxable value of their houses and land was to be determined according to *an Estimate of the net annual Value, (that is to say), of the Rent for which, one Year with another, the same might in its actual State be reasonably expected to let*

---

[54] *General Valuation of Rateable Property in Ireland, Co. of Cork, Barony of Kinalea, Unions of Bandon and Kinsale, 25 June 1851*, p. 12.

from Year to Year ... ."[55] Enumerated in 9 & 10 Vict. Cap. 110 were the "hereditaments" as defined in the Poor Law Act of 1838 that were to be valued: *"land, buildings, fisheries, canals, turf bog except when used by an occupier for fuel and manure."*[56] Exempt from the tax were churches and chapels, buildings used for education of the poor, burial grounds and cemeteries, infirmaries and hospitals, and public buildings such as court houses, jails and police barracks.

Furnished with a clean copy of the surveyor's perambulation book and maps, a valuator was dispatched to the land and began assessing his assigned district to determine the details for setting its poor rate. Accompanied by a spademan (a local laborer) who turned the soil for examination, the valuator proceeded to analyze it and enter in his book an estimate of its taxable value. Next, each building was examined verifying or modifying the measurements and the quality letter which had been assigned by the surveyor. The valuator entered in his book, when aware of it, any change of occupier or landlord since the surveyor's visit as well as any rents not already entered.

When the assessment of a civil parish was concluded, the valuator was instructed to sign, date and send his perambulation book and maps to Dublin.[57] This dating identifies the time period between completion of the valuation in the field and its eventual printing during which a change in occupier may have been noted by the researcher.

The Printed Poor Rate Valuation of 1846

When the Valuation Office staff had completed the necessary calculations, changes and corrections in the perambulation books for the civil parishes within a barony, the Commissioner of Valuation directed that a "list or table"[58] of the parishes, townlands and tenements in each poor law union within a barony be prepared for publication. Dated 15 June 1847 at the General Valuation Office, Dublin, the Barony of Balrothery West was the first barony of Griffith's Poor Rate Valuation to be printed in book form with blue paper covers. This tabulation provided the information essential for the Boards of Guardians of the two Unions of Balrothery and Dunshaughlin within the Barony to set their poor rates.

Note the two dates on the title page of the Barony of Balrothery West in figure 19 indicating when the valuation was printed (15 June 1847) and the date (3 September 1847) when appeals made against the valuations were to be heard by the Appeals Board. The dates may alert the researcher to extant parish registers, surviving census fragments, or other available sources for information about the people listed in the valuation.

---

[55] 9 & 10 Vict., Cap. 110, Section IX.
[56] Idem, Section LXIII.
[57] Idem, Section XIV.
[58]   9 & 10 Vict., Op. cit., Section XVI.

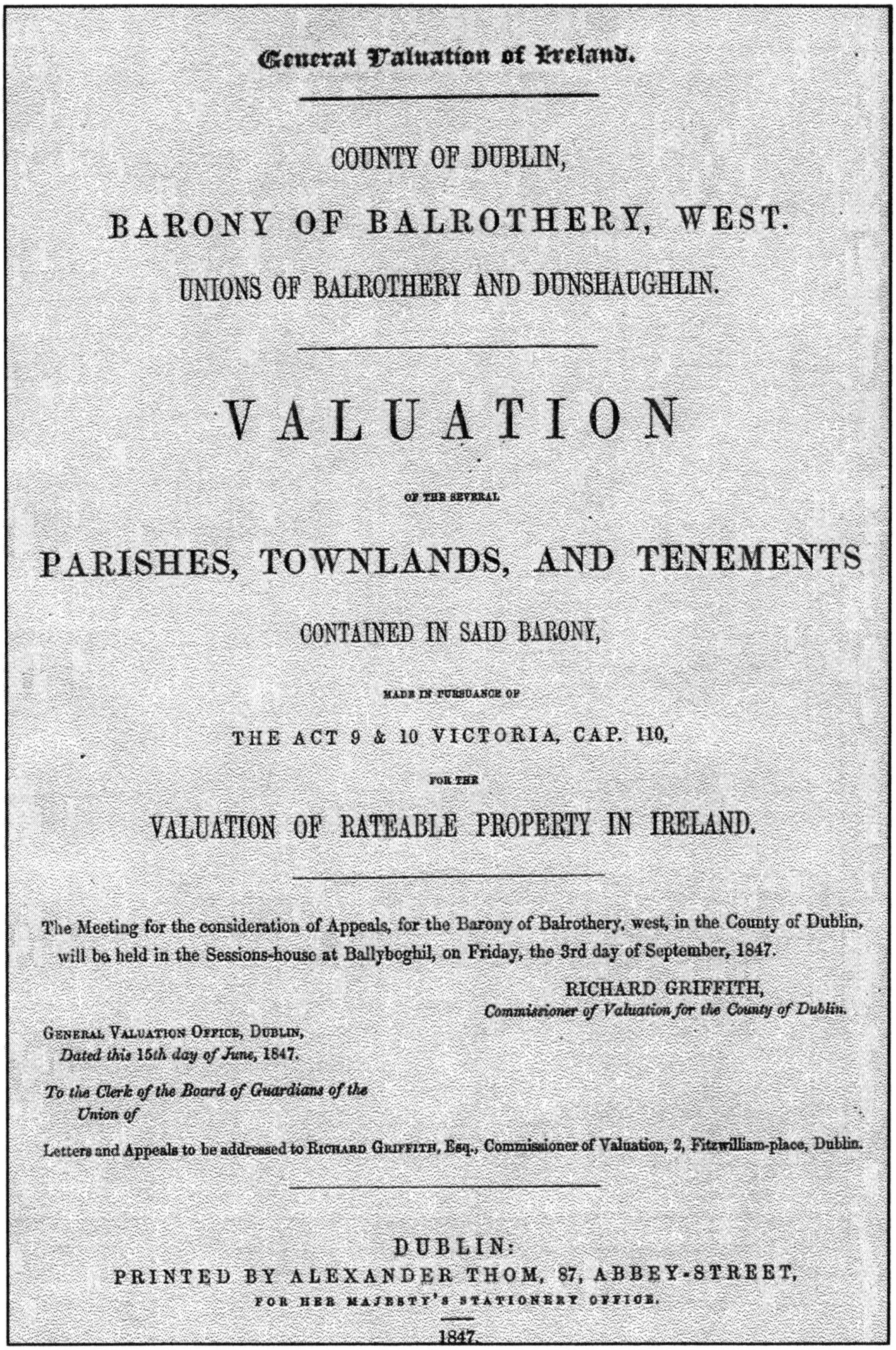

Figure 19. Title page of Barony of Balrothery West[59]

---

[59] From an original copy in the author's private collection.

Primary Valuation of Tenements.

COUNTY OF DUBLIN.

BARONY OF BALROTHERY WEST.

UNIONS OF BALROTHERY AND DUNSHAUGHLIN.

PARISH OF BALLYBOGHIL.

No. on Map.	Letter or No. in Field Book	Names of Townlands and Occupiers	Names of immediate Lessors	Description of Tenement	Content of Land. A. R. P.	Net Annual Value of Land. £ s. d.	Net Annual Value of Buildings. £ s. d.	Total Net Annual Value. £ s. d.
		BALLYBOGHIL.						
1	a	Patrick Seaver,	George Woods, Esq.,	House, offices, and land,	181 3 20	184 4 0	11 18 0	196 2 0
—	b	Edward M'Guinness,	Patrick Seaver,	House and yard,			1 12 0	1 12 0
2		Thos. or Peter Dungan,	George Woods, Esq.,	House, offices, and land,	66 0 26	66 18 0	5 1 0	71 19 0
3		Mary Connor,	George Woods, Esq.,	Land,	48 3 11	55 13 0		55 13 0
4	a	Phelim M'Cann,	Thomas Byrne,	House and land,	1 1 31	1 15 0	0 15 0	2 10 0
—	b	William M'Cann,	George Woods, Esq.,	House and yard,			0 11 0	0 11 0
5		Thomas Byrne,	George Woods, Esq.,	Land,	76 2 4	82 1 0		82 1 0
—	a	Bartholomew Ratty,	Thomas Byrne,	House and yard,			1 10 0	1 10 0
		Grave-yard,	George Woods, Esq.,	Grave-yard,	0 2 8	0 8 0		0 8 0
6	a	Mary Connor,	George Woods, Esq.,	House, offices, and land,	6 1 32	7 15 0	11 16 0	19 11 0
—	b	Patrick M'Cann,	George Woods, Esq.,	House and yard,			2 5 0	2 5 0
7	a	William M'Cann,	George Woods, Esq.,	Offices and land,	1 0 32	1 7 0	0 11 0	1 18 0
—	b	Peter Doran,	William M'Cann,	House and garden,	0 0 12	0 2 0	1 4 0	1 6 0
—	c	Michael Hand,	William M'Cann,	House and yard,			1 0 0	1 0 0
—	d	Catherine M'Cann,	William M'Cann,	House and yard,			0 19 0	0 19 0
—	e	James Sheil,	William M'Cann,	House and yard,			0 17 0	0 17 0
—	f	Elisabeth Hollywood,	William M'Cann,	House and yard,			0 16 0	0 16 0
8		Mary Sweetman,	George Woods, Esq.,	House, offices, & garden,	1 2 32	1 9 0	9 9 0	10 18 0
		Total,			384 3 8	401 12 0	50 4 0	451 16 0
		Exemptions: Grave-yard,			0 2 8	0 8 0	—	0 8 0
		Total, exclusive of exemptions,			384 1 0	401 4 0	50 4 0	451 8 0
		BELINSTOWN.						
1		Bartholomew Carthy,	Francis Delahoyde, Esq.	Land,	2 1 31	2 11 0	—	2 11 0
2		John Hamilton,	Francis Delahoyde, Esq.	House, offices, and land,	8 2 16	8 17 0	1 17 0	10 14 0
3		Thomas Byrne,	Sir Eyre Coote, Bart.,	Land,	44 2 6	47 1 0	—	47 1 0
4		James Bride,	Francis Delahoyde, Esq.	Land,	61 0 8	50 8 0	—	50 8 0
5		Francis Delahoyde, Esq.	In fee,	House, offices, and land,	100 1 0	86 18 0	4 0 0	90 18 0
6		Christopher Harford,	Francis Delahoyde, Esq.	House, offices, and land,	13 1 32	14 0 0	1 18 0	15 18 0
7		Peter Hewet,	Sir Eyre Coote, Bart.,	House, offices, and land,	108 1 24	96 7 0	5 13 0	102 0 0
		Total,			338 2 37	306 2 0	13 8 0	319 10 0
		CLONSWORDS.						
1	a	Andrew Macken,	George Woods, Esq.,	House, offices, and land,	58 1 3	60 9 0	23 7 0	83 16 0
—	b	Timothy Maguire,	Andrew Macken,	House,		—	1 13 0	1 13 0
		Total,			58 1 3	60 9 0	25 0 0	85 9 0
		DOOROGE.						
1		Christopher Sweetman,	George Woods, Esq.,	House, offices, and land,	94 2 11	97 7 0	8 6 0	105 13 0
2	a	Patrick Hamilton,	George Woods, Esq.,	House, offices, and land,	11 2 12	12 18 0	2 13 0	15 11 0
—	b	John Hamilton,	Patrick Hamilton,	House, offices, and yards,			1 12 0	1 12 0
3		Thomas Byrne, jun.,	George Woods, Esq.,	Land,	72 1 24	71 11 0	—	71 11 0
—	a	William Brennan,	Thomas Byrne, jun.,	House and yard,			1 4 0	1 4 0
—	b	Michael Thompson,	Thomas Byrne, jun.,	House and yard,			1 10 0	1 10 0
4		Thomas Byrne, sen.,	George Woods, Esq.,	House, offices, and land,	3 2 34	3 15 0	3 7 0	7 2 0
5		Patrick Harford,	George Woods, Esq.,	House, offices, and land,	3 3 37	4 0 0	1 0 0	5 0 0
6		Bartholomew Carthy,	George Woods, Esq.,	House, offices, and land,	16 3 19	19 1 0	4 17 0	23 18 0
		Total,			203 0 17	208 12 0	24 9 0	233 1 0

B

Figure 20. First page of Parish of Ballyboghil

Note in the first column of the Parish of Ballyboghil's tabulation (figure 20) a reference to the number on the surveyor's map and in the second column titled "Letter or No. in Field Book, " a reference to the perambulation book. In later printed valuations both map references will be combined in a single column. Notice also in the "Name of Townlands and Occupiers" column the absence of the Ordnance Survey Map number beneath the Townland Name routinely found in later valuations.

The printed version of the poor rate valuation is often titled "Primary Valuation of Tenements," "Primary" designates the valuation as *tentative* pending appeals against the poor rate assessments proposed by the Valuation Office. It is from this printing that the term "Griffith's Primary Valuation" frequently found in research literature originated. It is also the term that has created the erroneous, but understandable, impression that the valuation authorized by the 1846 Act was solely for the setting of the poor rates with no recognition of its application to the county cess.

When examining the manuscript and printed books of the six counties (Cork, Dublin, Kerry, Limerick, Tipperary, and Waterford), researchers will note that geographical areas of adjoining counties were also valued under the Act of 1846. When a portion of a Poor Law Union within one of the six counties extended into an adjoining county, it was valued as part of that county and given its own primary valuation book. A map of the Poor Law Unions in Co. Dublin[60] will show, for example, that part of the Poor Law Union of Celbridge is contained also in Co. Kildare and in Co. Meath. Thus, geographical areas of Clare, Carlow, Kildare, Kilkenny, Kings, Louth, Queens and Wicklow were valued along with the six counties.

The Poor Rate Appeal Process

Because 9 & 10 Vict., Cap. 110 provided a procedure for both landlord and occupier to appeal against the value placed on their holdings by the Valuation Office,[61] several hundred copies of the Primary Valuation were printed for distribution[62] to the Board of Guardians and to the local constabulary for circulation within the barony.[63] A notice was posted on a door of the Established Church building, the Roman Catholic chapel, and the Presbyterian Meeting House indicating the time and place where for twenty-eight days it could be examined. During this time an aggrieved ratepayer sent a signed notice of his intention to appeal with his reasons to the Clerk of his Board of Guardians. The Clerk in turn forwarded all such notices to the Commissioner of Valuation in Dublin who, if he found sufficient justification in the notices, assigned a valuator not involved in the primary valuation to reexamine the appealed tenements.

---

[60] Brian Mitchell, A New Genealogical Atlas of Ireland (Baltimore: Genealogical Publishing Co., Inc., 1986)
[61] 9 & 10 Vict., Op. cit., Section XXVIII.
[62] Select Committee), HC 1869 (362) IV, Op. cit., Question 53.
[63] Ibid, Question 53.

Furnished with the results of the check valuation, a Board of Appeals, chaired by two professional valuators appointed by Griffith, customarily met within forty days of the printed Primary Valuation to hear the persons aggrieved and to make decisions regarding their appeal. A subsequent printed version was issued enumerating modifications to the original valuation; its title page carries the wording "As Revised and Amended by the Sub-Commissioners of Valuation appointed under the Act 9 & 10 Vic. Cap. 110." Generally all tenements are shown along with the modifications made to those altered by the appeals board. Some revised printings, however, identify only the holdings for which the sub-commissioners rendered a change. If the sub-commissioners failed to settle an appeal to a holder's satisfaction during the hearing, the ratepayer was entitled to a further appeal before the Sessions of the Peace court which had the final decision in the matter.

In the early years of the Famine there was an incredible number of appeals to the primary valuation. In Co. Tipperary, for example, more than four thousand appeals were filed. Griffith believed that they were instigated by people attempting to discredit the valuation system. A great number of the appeals had been filed without the knowledge of the landlords and tenants themselves; when the appeals could not be sustained, the numbers decreased substantially.[64]

Landlords and tenants in many poor law unions did not file official notice to appeal the valuation of their holdings; often questions and concerns were settled informally by the Commissioner of Valuation or his representative without a formal appeals hearing ever taking place. A survey of the ninety-six primary valuation books completed under the 1846 Act identifies only thirty-four extant corresponding appeals books.[65]

Because some repositories do not have a complete set of the 9 & 10 Vict. primary valuation books, the title page of each book should be examined to ascertain whether it is a primary printing or a later revised appeals printing, since occupier names have been known to change even within the short time between their printing dates. An examination of the altered valuation book of the Parish of Ballyboghil shows two alterations between its primary valuation of 15 June 1847 and the altered printing of 15 May 1848. Holding No. 3 in the Townland of Ballyboghill shows an increase in Mary Connors' "Net Annual Value of Land," and holding No. 7b shows a change in occupier from Peter Doran to Peter Thornton.

---

[64] Select Committee, HC 1869 (362) IV, Op. cit., Question 1194.
[65] James R. Reilly CGRS, *An Inventory of the Books of Sir Richard Griffith's General Valuation of Rateable Property in Ireland,* (Salt Lake City, Utah: Redmond Press, 1998)

No. on Map	Letter or No. in Field Book	Names of Townlands and Occupiers	Names of Immediate Lessors	Description of Tenement	Content of Land			Net Annual Value of Land			Net Annual Value of Buildings			Total Net Annual Value		
					A.	R.	P.	£	s.	d.	£	s.	d.	£	s.	d.
		BALLYBOGHIL.														
1	a	Patrick Seaver,	George Woods, Esq.,	House, offices, and land,	181	3	20	184	4	0	11	18	0	196	2	0
–	b	Edward M'Guinness,	Patrick Seaver,	House and yard,				—			1	12	0	1	12	0
2		Thos. or Peter Dungan,	George Woods, Esq.,	House, offices, and land,	66	0	26	66	18	0	5	1	0	71	19	0
3		Mary Connor,	George Woods, Esq.,	Land,	48	3	11	48	15	0				48	15	0
4	a	Phelim M'Cann,	Thomas Byrne,	House and land,	1	1	31	1	15	0	0	15	0	2	10	0
–	b	William M'Cann,	George Woods, Esq.,	House and yard,				—			0	11	0	0	11	0
5		Thomas Byrne,	George Woods, Esq.,	Land,	79	2	4	82	1	0				82	1	0
–	a	Bartholomew Ratty,	Thomas Byrne,	House and yard,				—			1	10	0	1	10	0
–		Grave-yard,	George Woods, Esq.,	Grave-yard,	0	2	8	0	8	0				0	8	0
6	a	Mary Connor,	George Woods, Esq.,	House, offices, and land,	6	1	32	7	15	0	11	16	0	19	11	0
–	b	Patrick M'Cann,	George Woods, Esq.,	House and yard,				—			2	5	0	2	5	0
7	a	William M'Cann,	George Woods, Esq.,	Offices and land,	1	0	32	1	7	0	0	11	0	1	18	0
–	b	Peter Thornton,	William M'Cann,	House and garden,	0	0	12	0	2	0	1	4	0	1	6	0
–	c	Michael Hand,	William M'Cann,	House and yard,				—			1	0	0	1	0	0
–	d	Catherine M'Cann,	William M'Cann,	House and yard,				—			0	19	0	0	19	0
–	e	James Sheil,	William M'Cann,	House and yard,				—			0	17	0	0	17	0
–	f	Elizabeth Hollywood,	William M'Cann,	House and yard,				—			0	16	0	0	16	0
8		Mary Sweetman,	George Woods, Esq.,	House, offices, & garden,	1	2	32	1	9	0	9	9	0	10	18	0
		Total,			384	3	8	394	14	0	50	4	0	444	18	0
		Exemptions :														
		Grave-yard,			0	2	8	0	8	0		—		0	8	0
		Total, exclusive of exemptions,			384	1	0	394	6	0	50	4	0	444	10	0
		BELINSTOWN.														
1		Bartholomew Carthy,	Francis Delahoyde, Esq.	Land,	2	1	31	2	11	0		—		2	11	0
2		John Hamilton,	Francis Delahoyde, Esq.	House, offices, and land,	8	2	16	8	17	0	1	17	0	10	14	0
3		Thomas Byrne,	Sir Eyre Coote,	Land,	44	2	6	47	1	0		—		47	1	0
4		James Bride,	Francis Delahoyde, Esq.	Land,	61	0	8	50	8	0				50	8	0
5		Francis Delahoyde, Esq.	In fee,	House, offices, and land,	100	1	0	86	18	0	4	0	0	90	18	0
6		Christopher Harford,	Francis Delahoyde, Esq.	House, offices, and land,	13	1	32	14	0	0	1	18	0	15	18	0
7		Peter Howet,	Sir Eyre Coote,	House, offices, and land,	108	1	24	96	7	0	5	13	0	102	0	0
		Total,			338	2	37	306	2	0	13	8	0	319	10	0
		CLONSWORDS.														
1	a	Andrew Macken,	George Woods, Esq.,	House, offices, and land,	58	1	3	58	0	0	20	0	0	78	0	0
–	b	Timothy Maguire,	Andrew Macken,	House,		—			—		1	13	0	1	13	0
		Total,			58	1	3	58	0	0	21	13	0	79	13	0
		DOOROGE.														
1		Christopher Sweetman,	George Woods, Esq.,	House, offices, and land,	94	2	11	97	7	0	8	6	0	105	13	0
2	a	Patrick Hamilton,	George Woods, Esq.,	House, offices, and land,	11	2	12	12	18	0	2	13	0	15	11	0
–	b	John Hamilton,	Patrick Hamilton,	House, offices, and yards,				—			1	12	0	1	12	0
3		Thomas Byrne, jun.,	George Woods, Esq.,	Land,	72	1	24	71	11	0				71	11	0
–	a	William Brennan,	Thomas Byrne, jun.,	House and yard,				—			1	4	0	1	4	0
–	b	Michael Thompson,	Thomas Byrne, jun.,	House and yard,				—			1	10	0	1	10	0
4		Thomas Byrne, sen.,	George Woods, Esq.,	House, offices, and land,	3	2	34	3	15	0	3	7	0	7	2	0
5		Patrick Harford,	George Woods, Esq.,	House, offices, and land,	3	3	37	4	0	0	1	0	0	5	0	0
6		Bartholomew Carthy,	George Woods, Esq.,	House, offices, and land,	16	3	19	19	1	0	4	17	0	23	18	0
		Total,			203	0	17	208	12	0	24	9	0	233	1	0

Figure 21. Altered Valuation Book, Townland of Ballyboghil, Parish of Ballyboghill, Barony of Balrothery West[66]

[66] Family History Library, Salt Lake City, Utah, 941.5, R2g, Vol. 50.

Annual Revision of the 1846 Poor Rate Valuation

Once a tenement's valuation was set, provision was made for an annual revision of the assessment according to Section XXX of the 1846 Act: [67]

> *"for the necessary Alteration and Revision from Time to Time, in the cases of those Tenements the Limits whereof shall become altered, or whereof the Value shall be changed by any Building being erected thereon, or thrown down or destroyed ... . That within Ten Days after the First Day of February in each Year after the Completion[68] of any such Valuation every Collector of Poor Rates ... shall lay before the Board of Guardians ... a List of all the Tenements ... which shall require Revision for any of the Reasons aforesaid, and the Clerk of the Union shall transmit the same within Twenty Days from such First Day of February, to the Commissioner of Valuation, with the Opinion of the said Board of Guardians whether a Revision is necessary on account of such Changes or alterations ...."*

A discussion between Richard Griffith and the chairman of the 1869 Select Committee[69] is significant. Griffith acknowledged the accuracy of the chairman's question that *"For nine years after 1844 [when Griffith commenced the "tenement "valuation in Dublin and Tipperary] there was not a single county issued?"* [for rating purposes]. When challenged *"what was the office doing?"* Griffith responded that the *"tenement valuation was a much more detailed valuation"* [than the townland valuation] declaring that *"... after the work was done in the field there was a great quantity of detail to be done in the office."* Although the chairman was correct that no entire county had been issued to the Guardians for rating purposes during the nine year period, twenty individual unions, however, had been issued for that purpose as shown by an identifying asterisk in Appendix No.7.

The importance of this Committee exchange lies in the fact that, although the Act authorized an annual tenement revision for Cork, Dublin, Kerry, Limerick, Tipperary and Waterford, none ever took place.

Why then were there no annual revision documents for these twenty unions? Analysis of Section XXX of the Act gives a clue. The unions of County Dublin aside because of problems described above,[70] the earliest union released was Abbeyleix in Queens County on 30 January 1852. Assuming the Board of Guardians put its poor rate into effect, for example, by February 3rd of that year, the rate would remain in effect for one year - until the following 1st of February 1853. But less than six months before Abbeyleix was due to be revised, the 1846 Act was repealed and super-

---

[67] 9 & 10 Vict., Op. cit.,, Section XXX
[68] The date issued to the Board of Guardians for rating purposes.
[69] Select Committee, HC 1869 (362) IV, Op. cit., Question 1490-1495.
[70] Errors in the Dublin County valuations under 9 & 10 Vict. made them invalid for rating purposes.

seded by 15 & 16 Vict., Cap. 63. The last of the twenty unions that had been issued for setting poor rates was the Union of Tipperary on 24 December 1852. But the 1846 Act had been repealed six months earlier, and 15 & 16 Vict., Cap.63 was already in operation.

THE THIRD VALUATION: THE TENEMENT VALUATION ACT OF 1852

Although improvements had been made in establishing the Poor Law rates under the provisions of the Act of 1846, dissatisfaction remained among rate payers because they continued to be burdened with two systems of local taxation - county cess and poor rates. Parliament responded in June 1852 with "*one uniform Valuation of Lands and Tenements which may be used for all public and local Assessments and other Rating.* "[71] This third valuation was to remain in effect in the Republic of Ireland for 130 years until overturned by the High Court of Ireland in July 1982.

The Act of 1852 (15 & 16 Vict., Cap. 63) describes the transitional procedures to be implemented to attain the uniform taxation system:

> *1. Townland and Tenement Valuations issued prior to 30 June 1852 to a Grand Jury or Board of Guardians under the provisions of 6 & 7 Will., 4, Cap. 84 and 9 & 10 Vict., Cap. 110 for setting county cess and poor rates are to remain in force until revised under the provisions of the new Act of 1852.*
>
> *2. The valuation of any county currently in progress under 9 & 10 Vict., Cap. 110 is to proceed and upon completion is to be used for all taxation purposes, not solely for county cess and poor rate.*
>
> *3. The counties previously valued under the 1826 Townland Act (Appendix No. 5) are now to undergo a tenement valuation.*

To facilitate the new Act Griffith published for the use of his field and office staffs his third manual of guidelines titled *Instructions to the Valuators and Surveyors for the Uniform Valuation of Lands and Tenements in Ireland.* The guidelines were a compilation of the instructions issued in 1844 by the Lord Lieutenant and new directives issued up to 1853.[72] It was the most comprehensive of the guides and reflected the skills and techniques of land valuation developed in the field under his leadership during the twenty-two years since the initial valuation of Co. Londonderry.

The same kind of manuscript materials produced by the 1846 Act, the perambulation books and OS maps useful to the researcher, were continued by the 1852 Act.. The perambulation books of the 1852 Act are shared between the Valuation Office and the National Archives.

When a union's assessment was completed and checked in the field, the valuators' books and maps were sent to Dublin where maps were checked and calculations verified by the office staff, and the manuscript was finally sent to the printer. However, the printed version of each Poor Law Union was now published individually rather than being printed together with other baronial unions as in the earlier Act. Provision was made for sufficient copies of the printed primary valuation, usually between 200 and 250 copies, to be sent to the County Treasurer and to the Board of Guardians for distribution prior to the hearing of appeals.

---

[71] 15 & 16 Vict., Cap. 63.
[72] Select Committee, HC 1869 (362) IV, Op. cit., Question 904.

Although no Irish repository appears to have a complete set of the original printed valuation books, some extant copies are available for examination at the Dublin Valuation Office and at the Public Record Office of Northern Ireland.[73] Because their printed copies are in protective storage, the National Archives and the National Library of Ireland have microfiche copies of Griffith's for research use. The Family History Library, Salt Lake City, has an extensive, although incomplete, microfilm set of original volumes of the Republic and Northern Ireland as well as 146 bound originals or photocopies for the Republic.

The 1852 Act Appeals Process

Under the earlier 1846 Act revisions resulting from appeals to the primary valuation were printed in a second volume. However, under the Act of 1852 a major change took place because the Valuation Office did not print a second volume with appeal revisions due to its projected cost. Often overlooked by the researcher is a notice, usually printed in red ink, at the front of the primary valuation book that explains the new procedure.

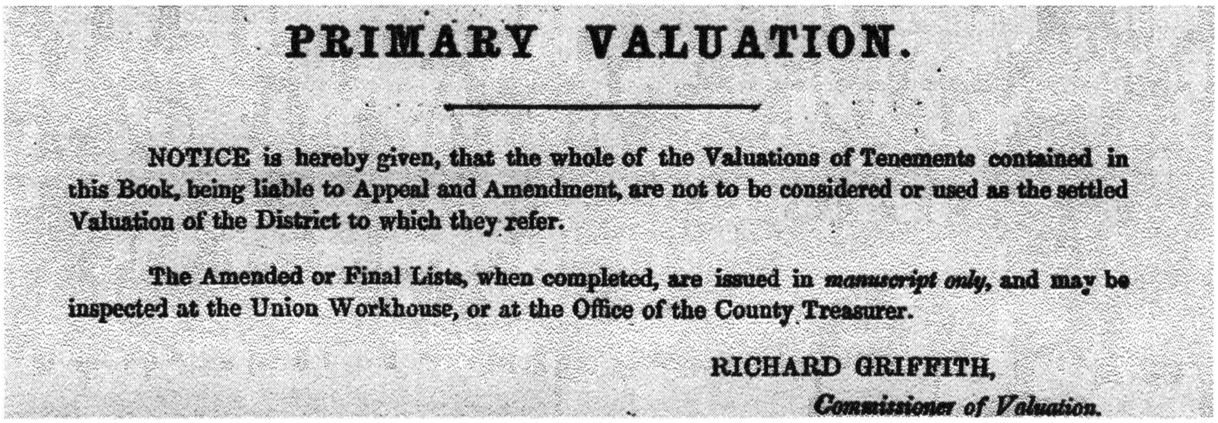

PRIMARY VALUATION.

NOTICE is hereby given, that the whole of the Valuations of Tenements contained in this Book, being liable to Appeal and Amendment, are not to be considered or used as the settled Valuation of the District to which they refer.

The Amended or Final Lists, when completed, are issued in *manuscript only*, and may be inspected at the Union Workhouse, or at the Office of the County Treasurer.

RICHARD GRIFFITH,
Commissioner of Valuation.

Figure 22. Red Notice

The *manuscript* edition is the finalized version of a union that reflects appeal modifications granted by the Commissioner of Valuation or the Court of Appeals. Three handwritten copies duplicating the eight column format of the primary valuation with an added column titled "Observations"were prepared. One copy was prepared for the County Treasurer for setting the grand jury cess, another copy was sent to the Board of Guardians to set the poor rates, and the third remained in the Valuation Office to serve as the master copy for all future adjustments to a union's valuation. These manuscript books of the 1852 Valuation Act are properly called "revision books."

---

[73] James R. Reilly CGRS, *An Inventory of the Books of Sir Richard Griffith's General Valuation of Rateable Property in Ireland,* (Salt Lake City, Utah: Redmond Press, 1998).

VALUATION OF TENEMENTS.
PARISH OF DRUMLUMMAN.

No. and Letters of Reference to Map.	Names.		Description of Tenement.	Area.			Rateable Annual Valuation.						Total Annual Valuation of Rateable Property.		
	Townlands and Occupiers.	Immediate Lessors.					Land.			Buildings.					
	POTTLEBANE— *continued.*			A.	R.	P.	£	s.	d.	£	s.	d.	£	s.	d.
19	James Smith,	Col. F. S. Greville,	Bog.	1	0	13	0	5	0	—			0	5	0
20	James Smith,	Same,	House, offices, and land,	8	1	3	6	0	0	0	10	0	6	10	0
21	James Smith (*Little*),	Same,	Bog.	0	3	28	0	3	0	—			0	3	0
22	James Cunningham,	Same,	House, offices, and land,	38	1	14	24	5	0	1	15	0	26	0	0
23	Thomas Murphy, sen.,	Same,	Bog.	0	3	23	0	3	0	—			0	3	0
24 *a & b*	Thomas Murphy, sen.,	Same,	House and land, and labourer's ho. & gar.	7	0	35	4	10	0	1	0	0	5	10	0
25	Thomas Murphy, jun.,	Same,	Bog.	1	1	34	0	2	0	—			0	2	0
26	Thomas Murphy, jun.,	Same,	House, offices, and land,	18	2	9	12	5	0	0	15	0	13	0	0
			Total,	271	1	39	175	5	0	15	0	0	190	5	0

Figure 23. Primary Valuation of the Townland of Pottlebane, Co. Cavan, printed 4 December 1855. Tenements numbered 19, 20 and 21 were the holdings of James Smith whose daughter Margaret married Thomas Reilly, the author's paternal great grandfather.

A second major change in the format of the manuscript book was made to facilitate the collection of taxes - the townlands of a union are grouped together by the electoral division to which each belonged rather than in the conventional civil parish arrangement of the primary valuation books.

Using the *Alphabetical Index to the Townlands and Towns of Ireland 1871*[74] the researcher easily places a townland within its electoral division. To locate the Family History Library microfilm of the *manuscript* valuation of an ancestor's tenement, search the locality catalog by " (Name of County) - Land and Property - Valuation Lists for (Name of County)." If the Rural District is not known, scan among the various 'Rural Districts' to find the desired electoral division.

```
TITLE
Valuation lists for Cavan County, Mullaghoran Rural District, 1857-1938.

PUBLICATION INFORMATION
Salt Lake City : Filmed by the Genealogical Society of Utah, 1970.

FORMAT
3 microfilm reels ; 35 mm.

NOTES
Microfilm of original records at the Ireland Valuation Office, Dublin.

CONTENTS
Indexed at beginning of each volume.
                                                              BRITISH
                                                              FILM AREA
v. 1-2  Electoral divisions:  Drumlumman ----------------- 0816835
                              Kilcogy
v. 3-4  Electoral divisions:  Kilgolagh ----------------- 0816836
                              Loughdawan
v. 5    Electoral division:   Scrabby ----------------- 0816837
```

Figure 24. Rural District of Mullaghoran, Electoral Division of Kilcogy, Co. Cavan
Family History Library Locality Catalog

---

[74] Family History Library microfilm # 0476999, item 2.

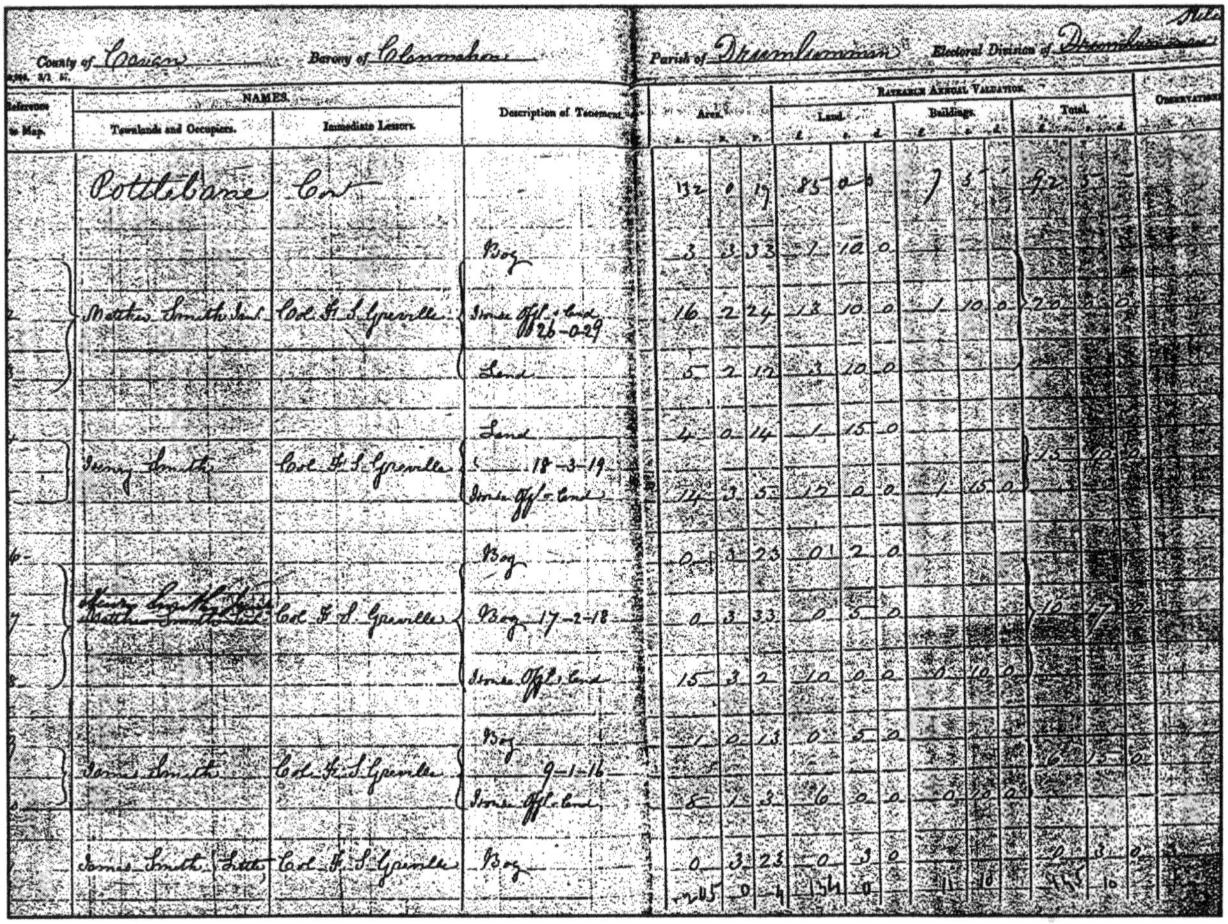

Figure 25. First Manuscript Revision Book of Townland of Pottlebane, Co. Cavan, dated 4 April 1857.
Family History Library, Film No. 0816835

Annual Revision of the 1852 Valuation

To carry out the annual revision of a tenement, 15 & 16 Vict., Cap. 63 provided " *... that within Ten Days after the First day of February in each Year after any such Valuation shall be completed and in operation every Collector of Poor Rates within each Poor Law Union ... shall make out and lay before the Board of Guardians ... a List of all the Tenements or Hereditaments situate within every Townland in the said Union which shall require Revision ... .* "[75]

The tax collector was expected to include on the list the change of an occupier's name, for example, because of death, migration, emigration, or a change of rate-payer, for example, from father to son or widow to son. The lessor from whom a holding was rented required a name change when the holding was sold or leased to a new landlord. When part of a farm was consolidated with another farm, the collector was expected to inform the Board of Guardians; similarly, when a farm was divided, he recorded a need for change on the list. Although consolidation and division of land

---

[75] 15 & 16 Vict., Cap 63, Section XXIX.

within a townland caused an increase or decrease in the assessment of an individual tenement, the total taxable value of the townland remained unchanged for fourteen years as specified in the Act.

Should a tax collector fail, accidentally or deliberately, to include a tenement that should be revised, any occupier within twenty days of the posting of the tax collector's list at the Workhouse was permitted to submit to the Board of Guardians a list of any tenement, including his own, that in his opinion should be revised.[76] This would seem to have been an opportunity for both small and large holders of land to keep their neighbors and tenants sensitive to even the smallest change in a holding that would affect rates.

After receiving a Board of Guardians' requested changes, it was the decision of the Commissioner of Valuation to either simply make the change, such as an occupier's name, or to send a valuator to the union to examine the requested change. After a decision had been made, a union's manuscript book and the Office copy were altered simply by cross-outs and write-overs. In succeeding years, according to a circular issued 1 November 1866 by the Valuation Office to the clerks of the unions and to the revising surveyors, "all alterations in the office book are to be carefully and neatly made ... and the date of the revision to be written on the margin [Observations column] in each instance. As far as practicable ink of a different colour should be used at each revision."[77]

Examination of early Valuation Office revision books will frequently show cross-outs and write-overs that are not dated nor in colored ink. It would appear that over time problems may have been experienced by the Office staff in keeping changes clear and accurate between the Office and the Board of Guardians resulting in the directive requiring a uniform system for alterations in both sets of books. As an illustration, the first Revision Book of Kilcogy Electoral Division which includes the townland of Pottlebane shows a number of undated changes in names, acreage and value; holding No. 17 has a change in occupier name, undated and in black ink. The earliest modifications in colored ink are dated "1863" in red ink in the second book for Kilcogy E.D.

In theory, after all alterations were made for the annual revision, a new set of three books reflecting the changes was to be prepared; but in actual practice, because of the time and expense involved, only the County Treasurer would receive a newly written copy each year. A Board of Guardian's book, on the other hand, was replaced about every three to five years[78]; in actual practice, some Office and Union books were used for ten years before being completely rewritten. However, note should be taken that the Clerk of the Mitchelstown Union reported to the 1869 Committee:

> *"The books consist of a number of leaves, a cover attached to them with a bit of tape running through the cover; as long as it is tied you may call it a book, but at*

---

[76] 15 & 16 Vict., Op. cit., Section XXIX.
[77] Select Committee , HC 1869 (362) IV, Appendix No. 4, page 235
[78] Select Committee, HC 1869 (362) IV, Op. cit., Question 2775.

any time you can knock it into leaves. It is a great mistake to suppose that they are new books at all; in making the revision they interline until the interlining can go no further. Then they have these new leaves and they put in one or two in place of the old ones. When a book goes down [from the Valuation Office to the Union]*, instead of its being a new book, it is merely an old one with a new leaf. ... I have been 10 or 12 years clerk of the union, and I have never received what I call a new book."[79]*

After a random number of years, the Office copy of the manuscript book would be declared "cancelled" due to excessive cross-outs and write-overs, and it was put in storage where it would be readily available when needed by the staff for reference purposes. As a consequence, Irish repository staffs and researchers interchangeably refer to the manuscript books as "revision books" or "cancelled books." In the 1960s the stored revision books were bound together, generally in reverse chronological order. The bound volumes usually contain as many as six to ten cancelled books[80]. They are an invaluable source for tracing an ancestral surname beyond the printed primary valuation date for two or more additional generations.

Knowledge of a union's primary valuation printing date, its issue date to the authorities for rating purposes, and the date of the first manuscript revision may prove useful to a researcher. As an illustration, the portion of the Carlow Union located in Co. Kildare was printed on 28 September 1850. Its manuscript copy was issued two years and four months later on 14 February 1853 (Appendix No. 7), and the 1852 Act required the tax to be set within thirty days of its receipt by the Board of Guardians, that is, March 14, 1853.[81] The tax was effective for approximately twelve months until the subsequent 1 February 1854 when the first annual revision was to begin. Thus 28 September 1850 to 1 February 1854 - a time span of three years and four months that could be a "black hole" of changes in occupier, lessor, and land consolidation and division. Such extended time lapses require further searches in church registers, estate papers and rent rolls, eviction documents, and workhouse records.

Another area of concern should be the accuracy of the revisions offered by the tax collector for forwarding to Dublin. It was reported by a Valuation Office staff member that *"the returns from the clerks of the unions would not average one-fifth of the changes that are discovered"* by the valuator sent to do revisions.[82] Several other witnesses indicated that the responsibility for reporting changes lay not only with the tax collector but also with the occupiers and lessors themselves who

---

[79]Ibid, Question 4493.
[80] Frances McGee, *National Archives Report on Records Held in the Valuation Office*, 1990.
[81] 15 & 16 Vict., Op cit., Section LII.
[82] Select Committee, HC 1869 (362) IV, Op. cit., Question 561.

had made any alterations in their holdings.[83] A grand jury member from Co. Limerick relates that " *So far from the Act being complied with as to the names of occupiers, I found in many cases the names of persons who had left years before still remaining on the books; the present occupiers were not put on, and the proper lessors were, in many cases, not put on.*"[84]

A further caution was expressed by the Clerk of Roscommon's Strokestown Union who stated that " *A collector does not go around searching for this information [changes in a tenement]; he only acquires it incidentally in the discharge of other duties.*"[85]

As the overall supervisor in the early years of the Tenement Valuation, Griffith had the assistance of an office superintendent who supervised the staff of 100 men in the field and in the Valuation Office. It was this staff that Griffith defended in his confrontation with the Select Committee chairman as being unable to expedite the valuation because of the magnitude of work needing to be performed. However, by 1853 his staff had grown to 300, and he now had the assistance of six office superintendents to supervise them. Each superintendent was assigned a number of counties whose daily valuation operations he supervised. Mr. Henry Duffy, for example, oversaw Counties Cavan, Fermanagh, Leitrim, Longford, Roscommon and Westmeath. Giving evidence before the 1869 Select Committee, his description of his responsibilities during a poor law union's revision gives a perception of the Valuation Office at that time period:

> "*I have to examine the documents when they come in after the revision is completed, and see what portions of these documents require to be replaced. The documents we have been using in previous revisions for three or four years, in consequence of a great many alterations or interlineations, sometimes require replacement. The office books I have replaced on an average every fourth year; the poor law guardians' copies every third year; and the county treasurers' copies every year, a full copy. The maps are redrawn every five years.*
>
> "*I have, during the interim between the two revisions, to register all complaints made to the office respecting valuations or applotments of previous revisions, and all applications for future revision. My assistants [clerks] check the computations of areas so complained against, and I make notes in all such cases, calling the future revising officer's attention to them.*
>
> "*When I receive the lists of cases for revision from the clerks of the unions (they are supplied once a year, immediately before the revisions), I classify the notes made by me, and attach them to the clerk's lists of the respective unions to which they relate.*

---

[83] Ibid, Question 562.
[84] Ibid, Question 1799.
[85] Ibid, Question 2913.

"I then make out a map of my district, comprising six counties ... . I have these maps lithographed ... and colour them; the time when the unions were revised the year before, and the officer [valuator] that revised them.

"I lay the map before the Commissioner; receive his instructions as to the district to be revised by each officer, and the consecutive order in which the revisions of the unions is to be carried out.

"When the Commissioner gives orders to have the revision commenced, the chief clerk sends the usual notices to the clerks of the unions, and to all parties who had, since the completion of the last revision, expressed a wish to be informed when the next revision of their property would take place.

"The dates of the issue of and of the receipt of all documents and the dates of issuing the valuations to the county treasurers, poor law guardians, Etc., are always registered by me, and the documents sent to the revisors are invoiced, and when returned, are checked and compared with the invoice, lest they should be lost during the field work. On receipt of the documents from the revisors, the lists for the poor law guardians and county treasurers are put in [clerks'] hands for correction and copying.

"While this is going on, the revision is carefully examined, the computations of areas, applotments, and totals are checked, and the alterations investigated by contrasting them with the previous revision or valuation."[86]

---

[86] Ibid, Question 1896.

A SOURCE OF GENEALOGICAL INFORMATION

The Public Record Office in Dublin's Four Courts building complex was destroyed on June 29, 1922 during the Irish Civil War. Among irreplaceable documents stored there were Ireland's census schedules of 1821 through 1851, wills and other probate records, and almost a thousand Church of Ireland parish registers. Although some few fragments of these records did survive, for family historians and genealogists their destruction is a great loss of information needed to construct relationships with their ancestors. The late onset in 1845 of the civil registration of Protestant marriages, the scarcity of Roman Catholic sacramental registers in the early years of the nineteenth century, and the long overdue civil registration of all birth, deaths and Catholic marriages in 1864 serve to underscore the often formidable challenges of Irish research.

The valuations undertaken in 1846 and 1852 are frequently described in genealogical literature as a "census substitute" for the years between the Great Famine and the start of civil registration in 1864. Although extensive in their listing of names, they are not the customary census enumeration of family members living in a household. However, in what appears on the surface to be a simple inventory of occupiers of taxable property in nineteenth century Ireland, genealogists will find a wealth of details to link family members and to lay bare clues for developing search strategies to overcome the 1922 loss of census, probate and church records.

The 1846 and 1852 printings of *The Valuation of Rateable Property in Ireland* are readily available in repositories world-wide, in public libraries, and in the LDS Family History Library and its Family History Centers. These volumes will be used to answer the question "Is there more in Griffith's than just names?"

Analysis of the Valuations reveals information about the economic conditions of an ancestor, and perhaps, siblings, relatives and in-laws. Houses and their adjacent structures are described and valued. An occupation is often revealed. Family relationships may be deduced. The absence of an ancestor's name within its pages is better understood when based on real knowledge rather than an uninformed "Oh, I guess they emigrated."

The Land and Its Tenancy

Much of the Act (8 Anne, Cap. 3) passed in 1709 during the reign of English Queen Anne dealt with the property rights of Catholics and was designed to deprive them of economic power and social position. Catholics were forbidden to buy land, to inherit or receive land as a gift from a Protestant, to hold a mortgage on land, or to hold a lease of more than thirty-one years or any lease that allowed the profits of the land to exceed one-third of the rent on the property.

With the gradual lessening of some of these restrictions and the enactment of the Catholic Emancipation Act in 1829, familiarity with the size of a tenement and how it was used - tillage, pasture, turbary, mill and so forth - will often classify the social and economic status of its occupier during the first half of the nineteenth century, the period of Griffith's valuations.

An occupier of five acres or less was generally designated as a cottier or laborer. He held his house and land "from year to year." Rent was frequently set by a landlord at an auction to the highest bidder among those seeking a holding. Often the laborer paid his rent by working on the landlord's land at 5 or 6 pence a day rather than paying with hard cash. Five acres or less of inferior soil were rented to these occupiers to raise food for their families, since landlords were often unwilling to let good land to a laborer.

An occupier holding between five and thirty acres was considered to be a "small" or "medium" farmer who usually paid his rent in cash. Small farmers frequently rented "from year to year," while medium farmers often had a lease for better quality land.

An occupier who held thirty or more acres was a "strong" farmer or grazer of livestock who held a favorable lease on the land.

Occasionally owners of large tracts of land were known to allow their land to become the haven and home of large numbers of "squatter" tenants during the famine years, or they were unaware that it had been overrun by such non-rent paying occupiers.

A lease document spelled out its length, the amount of land to be leased, and the rate of rent per acre. Other specifics stated whether the land was to be used for tillage or pasture, how often and in what manner the rent was to be paid, and the rights and duties of the tenant and landlord. A County Armagh lease dated 1779 required the lessee, his heirs and their under tenants to " *grind all their corn, malt, grain at one of the manor mills belonging to Lord Gosford [the landowner] and shall pay the toll thereof.* "[87]

The majority of leases for a stated period of time were either for thirty-one years or a "lease of lives." A lease of lives set its length by the number of years remaining in the lives of three individuals named in the lease and agreed upon by the landlord and tenant. Although not required, the three lives usually included the lessee, his youngest child and a third person. It was not unheard of for the third person to be the reigning monarch or a royal child. The lease remained in force and the rent agreement unchanged until the death of the last named person.[88]

Seeking Genealogical Information

Legislation required that Griffith describe, catalogue and value each tenement in a townland and publish the results in a volume entitled *General Valuation of Rateable Property in Ireland*. Today this publication is commonly referred to as "Griffith's Primary Valuation" or simply "Griffith's Valuation."

---

[87] Brian Mitchell, *Pocket Guide to Irish Genealogy*. (Baltimore: Clearfield Co., 1991, page 45.)
[88] Thomas de Moleyns. Esq., *The Landowner and Agent's Practical Guide*, (Dublin: Hodges, Smith and Co., 1860.)

The printed version of the civil parish of Usk (figure 26), printed on 14 September 1853, summarizes in its eight columns the voluminous details gathered for each tenement or holding by his surveyors and valuators in the fields and streets, in the bogs and mountains, in the towns and villages of this mid-nineteenth century civil parish:

1. Number and letter of Reference to Map
2. Names of Townlands and Occupiers
3. Names of Immediate Lessors
4. Description of Tenement

5. Area in Acres, Roods, Perches
6. Rateable Annual Valuation of Land
7. Rateable Annual Value of Buildings
8. Total Annual Value

COUNTY OF KILDARE.

BARONY OF NARRAGH AND REBAN, EAST.

UNION OF NAAS.

PARISH OF USK.

No. and Letters of Reference to Map		Names		Description of Tenement	Area	Rateable Annual Valuation		Total Annual Valuation of Rateable Property
		Townlands and Occupiers	Immediate Lessors			Land.	Buildings.	
					A. R. P.	£ s. d.	£ s. d.	£ s. d.
		BALLYMOUNT. (Ord. S. 32.)						
1	a	James Leigh,	John La Touche,	House, offices, and land,	92 1 28	44 0 0	3 0 0	47 0 0
—	b	James Kenna,	Same,	House,			0 5 0	0 5 0
2 A		Patrick Mape,	Same,	Land,	2 0 24	0 15 0		
— B				House, office, and land,	2 0 24	0 15 0	0 10 0	2 0 0
3 A		Patrick Brien,	Same,	House, office, and land,	1 0 23	0 10 0	0 10 0	
— B				Land,	4 0 38	1 10 0		2 10 0
4		Patrick Murphy,	Same,	House and land,	1 1 3	0 15 0	0 10 0	1 5 0
5		Martin Coleman,	Same,	House and land,	1 1 34	0 15 0	0 10 0	1 5 0
6	a	Patrick Connor,	Same,	House and land,	3 1 28	1 15 0	0 5 0	2 0 0
—	b	Judith M'Gear,	Patrick Connor,	House,			0 5 0	0 5 0
—	c	Vacant,	Same,	House,			0 5 0	0 5 0
7		Thomas Toole,	John La Touche,	House and land,	1 2 34	1 0 0	0 10 0	1 10 0
8 A	a	John Keatley,	Same,	Land,	23 3 6	6 0 0		39 15 0
— B				House, offices, and land,	58 2 15	32 0 0	1 15 0	
—	b	John Cleary,	John Keatley,	House,			0 5 0	0 5 0
—	c	Michael Byrne,	Same,	House,			0 5 0	0 5 0
—	d	Mary Connor,	Same,	House,			0 5 0	0 5 0
9 A		Michael Butterfield,	Henry Carroll,	Land,	5 2 21	3 5 0		4 5 0
— B					1 2 32	1 0 0		
—	A a	Bridget Murphy,	Same,	House and garden,	0 1 8	0 4 0	0 5 0	0 9 0
10	a	Michael Brennan,	Same,	House, offices, and land,	6 3 26	3 15 0	1 0 0	4 15 0
—	b	Eliza Murphy,	Same,	House and garden,	0 2 2	0 8 0	0 10 0	0 18 0
11	a	William Valentine,	Same,	House, offices, & garden,	0 2 3	0 5 0	0 10 0	0 15 0
—	b	Denis Owen,	Same,	House, office, & garden,	0 3 28	0 10 0	0 5 0	0 15 0
—	c	Michael Owen,	Same,	House and garden,	0 0 21	0 2 0	0 5 0	0 7 0
12		Thomas Kelly,	Same,	House, office, and land,	14 0 0	7 10 0	0 15 0	8 5 0
13		Matthew Byrne, jun.	Same,	House, offices, and land,	27 0 35	13 5 0	1 0 0	14 5 0
14 A		Matthew Byrne,	Same,	Land,	27 3 13	15 0 0		15 0 0
— B			John La Touche,		8 0 18	5 5 0		5 5 0
15		Edward Leigh,	Henry Carroll,	House and land,	2 0 5	0 15 0	0 10 0	1 5 0
16		Matthew Butterfield,	Same,	House, offices, and land,	10 0 13	4 10 0	0 15 0	5 5 0
17		John La Touche,	In fee,	Land (bog),	17 0 10	0 5 0		0 5 0
				Total,	315 0 38	145 14 0	14 15 0	160 9 0
		BREWEL, EAST, or MERVILLE. (Ord. S. 32.)						
1	a	John Gorman,	Marmaduke C. Roberts,	House, office, and land,	34 1 10	16 5 0	1 0 0	17 5 0
—	b	Anne Dunne,	Same,	House,			0 5 0	0 5 0
—	c	Anne Dunne, jun.	Same,	House,			0 5 0	0 5 0
—	d	Vacant,	John Gorman,	House and office,			0 10 0	0 10 0
—	e	Edward Murphy,	Same,	House,			0 5 0	0 5 0
2		Ellen Harrington,	Marmaduke C. Roberts,	House, offices, and land,	112 3 22	55 10 0	3 0 0	58 10 0
—	b	Vacant,	Ellen Harrington,	House,			0 5 0	0 5 0
3		Patrick Doyle,	Marmaduke C. Roberts,	House, offices, and land,	22 1 22	9 10 0	0 10 0	10 0 0
4		Robert M'Loughlin,	Same,	House, offices, and land,	36 3 1	14 10 0	1 5 0	15 15 0
5		Robt. M'Loughlin, jun.	Same,	House, offices, and land,	24 1 33	8 10 0	0 10 0	9 0 0
6		William M'Loughlin,	Same,	House, offices, and land,	24 3 38	9 0 0	1 0 0	10 0 0

Figure 26. Townland of Ballymount, Parish of Usk, Co. Kildare.

Ballymount is the first townland listed within the civil parish of Usk under the column headed **Townlands and Occupiers.** This column serves to identify the geographical address of each occupier of a tenement within its boundaries. Ballymount townland consists of seventeen holdings, each distinguished by an arabic number in the column headed **No. and Letters of Reference to Map.** In rural areas the number represents the order in which the valuator listed each holding in his perambulation book. The lot number does not necessarily signify the proximity of holdings to each other. Proximity can be determined only by examination of the Ordnance Survey map carried by the surveyor as he measured and marked each holding's boundaries on it; the map shows the perambulation book's corresponding numbers and letters. However, in a town and city the numbers do represent the holdings consecutively adjoining each other on streets and lanes.

The *Instructions* manual states that "when a cottagers' houses and gardens are included within the limits of a farm, the farmer's house ... should have the *italic* letter *a* prefixed to the number of the lot in which it is situated; the cottagers' [houses should have] *b, c, &.*[89]" We learn from this instruction that holding No. 1 in Ballymount contains two houses; the first is occupied by James Leigh, a farmer, and the second by James Kenna, a cottager or agricultural worker on his farm.

The **Names of Immediate Lessors** indicates that Leigh and Kenna individually have John La Touche as their landlord and pay their rent to him. Although there is no specific information given as to the kind and length of tenure held by the two tenants, we may reasonably infer their tenure from the **Area** column which describes the size of each man's holding.

The size of a holding was frequently used as a rule of thumb to characterize Ireland's agricultural classes. The holder of less than five acres was labeled a 'cottier or laborer'; small farmers usually held between five and thirty acres, and the large farmer occupied more than thirty acres. Consequently, Leigh's "92 acres, 1 rood, 23 perches" would most certainly class him as a financially independent large farmer holding under a 'lease of years or lives,' while Kenna's house, for which no land area is taxed and whose value is a low 5 'shillings' in the **Rateable Annual Valuation of Buildings** column, is probably rented on a 'yearly tenancy' from John La Touche.

Contrary to common belief, a yearly tenant could not just be thrown off his or her holding by force, nor could the rent be raised at the mere whim of the landlord. The law

---

[89] Richard Griffith, *Instructions the Valuators and Surveyors appointed under the 15th and 16th Vict., c. 63, for the Uniform Valuation of Lands and Tenements in Ireland.1852,* Section 26. (Dublin: Alexander Thom, 1852).

presumed that a yearly tenancy persisted unchanged from year to year; it did not automatically expire at the end of a year but continued from year to year unless surrendered by the tenant. If the landlord wanted to change the tenancy, he could do so only by going into court. Once, therefore, a yearly tenancy was established, it could be changed only by mutual consent or litigation.[90]

Holding No. 6 shows that one of the two occupiers is both a tenant and a landlord. Patrick Connor rents three acres, one rood and thirty-four perches from John La Touche on which holding there are three houses. Connor himself occupies the **a** house and rents as landlord the **b** house to Judith McGear with the **c** house vacant and not creating income for him.

The landlord reference for holding No. 8 indicates that this 81+ acre farm is rented by John Keatley from John La Touche and, according to the map reference column, is divided into two 'quality lots' labeled A and B. Although Keatley's use of the 23 acre lot A, valued at approximately five shillings per acre, is not described as to its soil quality, it appears not to be of as good a quality as the 58 acres valued at approximately eleven shillings per acre. Examination of the perambulation book in Dublin's Valuation Office may confirm lot A's use for pasture and B's for crops.

Notice that Holding No. 9 shows two lots but does not record a house for occupier Michael Butterfield on either lot, although lot A does show a house and garden occupied by Bridget Murphy. Is he related to Bridget Murphy and does he reside in her house? Is he related to the Matthew Butterfield occupying holding No. 16 and does he live with him? Does he have a house in another townland? When an occupier holds land or other property in one townland but lives in another townland, the *Instructions* manual requires that his townland of residence be noted next to his name in the first holding's **Occupier** column.[91] For example, if he lived in the townland of Merville, Michael Butterfield would be listed in Ballymount as "Michael Butterfield (*Merville*)." Since there is no such notation, we can only conclude that he resides in Ballymount. But with whom?

The simple cartoon sketch in Figure 27 is designed to illustrate the **No. and Letters of Reference to Map** and the **Description of Tenement** columns for holdings numbered 1, 6, 8 and 9.

---

[90] W.E. Vaughn, *Landlords and Tenants in Ireland 1848-1904* . (Dublin: The Economic and Social History Society of Ireland, Rev. ed. 1994).
[91] Richard Griffith 1852, op. cit., Section 34.

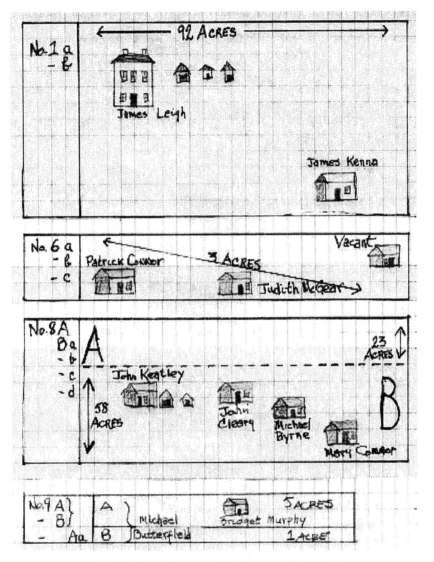

Figure 27. Sketch of Townland of Ballymount

Rundale Occupancy in the Valuation

The townland of Derreen, Co. Galway, shown in Figure 28 illustrates the subdivision of a single tenement by a group of tenants holding a 641+ acre parcel of land in common. Under the terms of the system, each tenant occupies a portion of the holding for a house and tillage use, but each tenant is financially responsible along with his fellow tenants for the full rent due on the entire holding. Should one or more of the occupiers fail to pay his rent, that share must be paid by the others. Although a widespread system of land occupancy before the Great Famine, consolidation of small holdings in the years following the Famine resulted in a limited number of rundale holdings in the Tenement Valuation. While it is not justifiable to assume that any of the thirteen occupiers in Derreen are related by blood or marriage, the presence of Michael and James Granaham, of John and James

Sheridan along with a Carey, a McHale and the others within this rundale communal setting strongly suggests an investigation of all surnames for possible familial relationships.

	DERREEN. (Ord. S. 46, 47, 58, & 59.)		Description of Tenement	A. R. P.	£ s. d.	£ s. d.	£ s.
a	Michael Granahan,	Sir W. Roger Palmer, Bt.	Land, house, & office,		5 0 0	0 15 0	5 15
b	James Granahan,	Same,	Land, house, & office,		3 0 0	0 15 0	3 15
c	Patrick Carey,	Same,	Land and house,		1 5 0	0 10 0	1 15
d	James M'Hale,	Same,	Land and house,		2 5 0	0 10 0	2 15
e	John Miles,	Same,	Land and house,		1 5 0	0 5 0	1 10
f	John Sheridan,	Same,	Land, house, & office,		6 0 0	0 15 0	6 15
g	Anthony Barrett,	Same,	Land and house,	641 0 29	3 0 0	0 5 0	3 5
h	James Sheridan,	Same,	Land and house,		3 5 0	0 10 0	3 15
i	James Mangan,	Same,	Land and house,		0 15 0	0 5 0	1 0
j	John Philips,	Same,	Land and house,		1 15 0	0 5 0	2 0
k	James Clarke,	Same,	Land and house,		1 0 0	0 5 0	1 5
l	Thomas Daly,	Same,	Land & herd's house,		2 5 0	0 5 0	2 10
m	Timothy Mulheran,	Same,	Land and house,		3 10 0	0 10 0	4 0
			Total,	641 0 29	34 5 0	5 15 0	40 0

Figure 28. Townland of Derreen, Co. Galway, Rundale Occupancy

Building Structures

The thatched cottage of Inishfree idealized in the John Wayne and Maureen O'Hara classic movie *The Quiet Man* with its brightly painted door and window trim and its lush flower garden is not the cottage of the ordinary farmer and laborer of mid-nineteenth century Ireland. The **Description of Tenements** column, although concise in wording, will reveal considerable information about an ancestor's economic condition during a tragic mid-century of famine and emigration.

Griffith's manual describes two classes of buildings, those used for houses and those used for offices. "House" includes all buildings used permanently as dwellings and all public buildings such as houses of worship, courthouses, schools and the like. "Office" includes factories, mills, shops and farm buildings such as a stable, turf shed, cow barn, corn shed, a piggery and so forth. Occasionally these farm buildings are referred to as "outhouses;" this term does not mean "sanitary facilities." Such structures, if they existed, were not taxable!

As described in the **Description of Tenement** column, a holding consisted typically of a "house, office and land," or a "house and land" or a "house and garden." A garden ordinarily described a small plot of ground used to raise food, be it in a rural area, town or city; it was not a flower bed.

Simply stated, the taxable value of a building structure was an estimate of the annual rent a landlord could reasonably expect from a responsible tenant. Construction materials, age, state of repair and dimensions of the house or office were the factors used to determine its taxable value. A house built of stone and brick in perfect repair with a slated roof is rated at a higher value than one constructed with mud walls roofed with thatch. The house of mud walls, thatched roof and needing repair is still rated higher than the dilapidated, scarcely habitable structure euphemistically called a cottage.

The Use of Agnomens

For the genealogist the *agnomen* has become one of the most useful clues for developing family relationship hypotheses when researching the Tenement Valuation. Section 31 of the *Instructions* manual states that when "*two or more persons in a townland have the same Christian name and surname, it will be necessary to obtain an agnomen (as Farmer).*" Agnomen is a Latin word meaning "an additional name." When Griffith offered the word "Farmer" as his sole example of an agnomen, he afforded great latitude to the valuators and surveyors in their choice of additional names to differentiate between individuals.

1. "**Junior - Senior**" as in figure 29 appears to be the most commonly utilized agnomen. Black's *Law Dictionary*[92] defines "junior" as "a convenient distinction between a father and son of the same name." Occasionally either "junior" or "senior" is omitted from the corresponding given and surname as is seen in figure 30. It is the author's contention that the singular use country-wide of "junior - senior" to distinguish between individuals, in spite of the array of agnomens available in each geographical locality, is a strong affirmation of a "father - son" relationship.

Figure 29. Junior - Senior

Figure 30. Senior agnomen omitted

---

[92] Henry Campbell Black, *Law Dictionary: Definitions of the Terms and Phrases of American and English Jurisprudence, Ancient and Modern* (St. Paul, MN, Henry Campbell Black, 4th ed., 1968).

2. The men employed by Griffith as valuators were native-born Irish familiar with the traditional naming practices. As seen in figure 31, the Gaelic practice of using a **father's name** to identify men with the same given name was a frequently applied agnomen. Use of the father's name in this fashion should not be interpreted to indicate that the father is deceased; he may be living in the same townland or in a neighboring one.

			CLARBALLY. (Ord. S. 9.)														
1			Thos.M'Govern(*Frank*)	George Finlay,	.	.	Office and land.	.	1	3	39	0	16	0	0	4	0	1	0	0
	{ a		Elizabeth M'Golrick,				House and land,					1	1	0	0	4	0	1	5	0
2	{ b		Patrick M'Govern (*Deinvilla*),	Same,	.	.	House,offices,& land.	19	3	28									
											5	5	0	1	5	0	6	10	0
3			Thos. M'Govern (*Tom*)	Same,	.	.	House, offices,and land,	18	0	4	6	15	0	1	5	0	8	0	0
4			Patk. M'Govern (*Tom*),	Same,	.	.	House,offices, and land,	15	3	32	6	0	0	0	15	0	6	15	0
5	{	Hugh M'Govern (*Hugh*), Owen M'Govern,		Same,	.	.	House,offices, & land, Offices and land,	23	2	18	6	10	0	1	0	0	7	10	0
											2	10	0	0	15	0	3	5	0
6			Hugh M'Govern(*Patk*)	Same.	.	.	House, offices,and land.	28	0	39	9	15	0	1	5	0	11	0	0
7			Patk. M'Govern(*Hugh*),	Same,	.	.	House,offices, and land,	35	2	0	14	0	0	1	10	0	15	10	0
8			Hugh M'Govern,	Same,	.	.	Land,	.	2	1	34	1	2	0	—			1	2	0
							Total,	.	145	2	34	53	14	0	8	3	0	61	17	0

Figure 31. Father's Given Name

In Clarbally townland (figure 31) there are eight holdings each listing a M'Govern occupier, five of whom are distinguished by a father's given name. What is the possibility that the four fathers (Frank, Tom, Patk., Hugh) are brothers? If so, the five men are cousins. Is it possible that one or more of the five is named for a paternal or maternal grandfather?

Deinvilla, a Gallic word, distinguishing Patrick M'Govern in Holding No. 2b indicates that his actual place of residence is in the adjoining townland of Deinvilla (Derryvella).[93]

There are baptismal and marriage records for the Roman Catholic parish serving Clarbally for the early 1820s that reveal a number of M'Governs named Thomas, Patrick, Hugh and Francis. There are also M'Golrick names in the registers. Is there a relationshp between M'Govern and M'Golrick occupiers in Clarbally and Derryvella?

3. In the townland of Kilmacduane West, figure 32, "Ellen" is used as an agnomen to distinguish John Cullinan from another John Cullinan whose agnomen is "Pat." The author submits that Ellen is the **widow** of John's father whose given name would have been used had he been living when the holding was valued. Were "Pat" and Ellen's deceased husband brothers, cousins? A second example in the townland is "Mary" and "Michael" to separate the two "John Honan." Possible relationships?

---

[93] Richard Griffith, op. cit., Section 34.

		KILMACDUANE, WEST. (Ord. Ss. 47, 48, 57, & 58.)														
45	a	John Cullinan (*Pat.*) .	Same,	.	. House, office, and land,	29	0	36	13	5	0	0	15	0	14	0	0
—	b	John Cullinan (*Ellen*),	Same,	.	. House, office, & garden,	0	0	6	0	1	0	0	9	0	0	10	0
—	c	Matthew Honan, .	Same,	.	. House, office, & gardens,	0	0	22	0	2	0	0	8	0	0	10	0
—	d	James Walsh, .	Same,	.	. House, office, & gardens,	0	0	20	0	2	0	0	8	0	0	10	0
—	e	John Honan (*Mary*), .	Same,	.	. House and garden,	0	0	34	0	3	0	0	12	0	0	15	0
—	f	Michael Honan,	Same,	.	. Ho., offices, & gardens,	0	0	20	0	1	0	0	14	0	0	15	0
46	}					4	0	26	2	0	0	—			}		
47		John Cullinan (*Pat.*) .	Same,	.	. Land, . .	16	0	39	4	15	0	—			7	15	0
48						2	0	5	1	0	0	—					
—	a	Michael Cullinan, .	Same,	.	. House, . .	—			—			0	2	0	0	2	0
49		John Cullinan (*Pat.*) .	Same,	.	. Land, . .	5	3	21	2	15	0	—			2	15	0
50						10	0	12	2	0	0	—					
51	}	John Honan (*Michael*),	Same,	.	. House, office, & land,	6	2	4	3	0	0	—			9	10	0
52						1	0	23	0	12	0	—					
53	a					6	3	20	3	8	0	0	10	0			

Figure 32. Widowed Mother's Maiden Name

4. Figures 33, 34 and 35 are examples of an **occupation, a physical characteristic and topography** as agnomens.

		ARNAGHAN. (Ord. S. 30 & 36.)														
1	a & b	Daniel Leddy, .	Henry Dopping,	.	House, offices, land, and cottier's house,	47	3	26	13	15	0	1	15	0	15	10	0
2		Patrick Reilly, .	Same,	.	House, offices, and land,	10	1	17	4	10	0	0	10	0	5	0	0
3		Patrick Reilly (*weaver*),	Same,	.	House, office, and land,	11	2	24	3	10	0	0	5	0	3	15	0
4		Bernard Duffy, .	Same,	.	House, offices, and land,	87	3	39	45	0	0	3	10	0	48	10	0
5		Anne M'Cabe, .	Same,	.	House, offices, and land,	14	2	8	8	15	0	0	15	0	9	10	0
6		Owen M'Glede, .	Same,	.	House, offices, and land,	14	3	12	8	5	0	0	15	0	9	0	0
					Total, .	195	1	8	83	15	0	7	10	0	91	5	0

Figure 33. Occupation

		COMINCH. (Ord. S. 37.)												
	a	Michael O'Horo, .	Sir W. Roger Palmer, Bt.,	Land, house, & office,				3	10	0	0	10	0	4	0	0
	b	Michael Ruane, .	Same,	Land, house, & office,				3	0	0	0	10	0	3	10	0
	c	Anthony Ruane (*Black*),	Same,	Land, house, & office,				3	0	0	0	10	0	3	10	0
1	d	Anthony Ruane (*White*),	Same,	Land, house, & office,	333	2	0	3	10	0	0	10	0	4	0	0
	e	Mary Maley, .	Same,	Land, house, & office,				4	5	0	0	10	0	4	15	0
	f	Bridget Ruane, .	Same,	Land, house, & office,				4	5	0	0	10	0	4	15	0
	—	Thomas Ruane, .	Same,	Land, . .				4	5	0	—			4	5	0
				Total, .	333	2	0	25	15	0	3	0	0	28	15	0

Figure 34. Physical Characteristic (Hair Color)

No.	Names	Immediate Lessors	Description	A R P	£ s d	£ s d	£ s d
	BEHY. *(Ord. S. 24 & 30.)*						
9			Land,	7 0 8	3 5 0	...	
10	John Reilly *(Hollow)*,	Same,	Land,	1 3 24	0 15 0	—	
11			House, offices, and land,	7 3 38	4 10 0	0 10 0	} 9 10 0
12			Land,	0 2 32	0 10 0	—	
13	Philip Reilly,	Same,	Land,	12 0 23	7 10 0	—	
14			House, offices, and land,	9 1 35	4 0 0	0 15 0	} 12 5 0
15	John Lang, John Reilly *(Hill)*, John Reilly *(Hollow)*, Philip Reilly,	Same,	Land,	3 2 13	0 15 0 / 0 15 0 / 0 7 0 / 0 7 0	—	0 15 0 / 0 15 0 / 0 7 0 / 0 7 0
16	John Coyle,	Same,	House, offices, and land,	5 1 18	2 15 0	0 10 0	3 5 0

Figure 35. Topography

5. Valuators did not confine the junior - senior agnomen to men. Figure 36 illustrates the female **junior - senior**. However, the agnomen does not necessarily signify a mother - daughter relationship; it may indicate a daughter-in-law relationship.

Note also the occupiers of Holding Nos. 1b and 8. Is the same Owen Farrelly occupying two houses? Is this a failure by the valuator to identify a father and son? Is it possible that the Thomas and Owen on Holding No.1b are father and son and that the Owen on No.8 is a grandson?

No.		Names	Immediate Lessors	Description	A R P	£ s d	£ s d	£ s d
		CORRYROURKE. *(Ord. S. 40.)*						
1	{ a	Thomas Farrelly,	Richard Fox,	House, office, & land,	15 3 20	3 15 0	0 10 0	4 5
	{ b	Owen Farrelly,		House, office, & land,		3 15 0	0 10 0	4 5
2		Andrew Carolan,	Same,	House and land,	1 0 30	0 5 0	0 5 0	0 10
3		Patrick Smyth,	Same,	Land,	5 3 34	3 5 0	—	3 5
–	a	Mary Sheridan,	Patrick Smyth,	House and sm. garden,	—		0 5 0	0 5
4	}	Peter Daly,	Richard Fox,	House, offices, and land,	19 3 15	11 0 0	0 15 0	} 12 15
5				Land,	1 2 14	1 0 0	—	
6		Mary Farrelly, jun.,	Same,	House and land,	1 0 2	0 15 0	0 5 0	1 0
7		Mary Farrelly,	Same,	House and land,	2 2 34	1 15 0	0 10 0	2 5
8		Owen Farrelly,	Same,	House, offices, and land,	7 2 1	3 15 0	0 10 0	4 5
9		Joseph Brady,	Same,	House, office, and land,	11 1 10	6 5 0	0 15 0	7 0

Figure 36. Female Use of Junior - Senior

6. When women bearing the same given and married surnames were widowed, the distinction between them was clarified by the use of their **maiden names** as an agnomen, figure 37.

No.			Names	Immediate Lessors	Description	A R P	£ s d	£ s d	£ s d
			KILNAMACK, EAST. *(Ord. S. 1.)*						
1	A a	B	Patrick Shanahan,	Earl of Donoughmore,	House, offices, and land,	74 3 37	71 18 0	3 12 0	75 10
–		b	William Connolly,	Earl of Donoughmore,	House,	—	—	0 7 0	0 7
–	B	a	Cornelius Callaghan,	Earl of Donoughmore,	House and yard,	...	—	0 16 0	0 16
2			John Bagwell, Esq.	In fee,	Land,	239 0 30	114 19 0	—	114 19
–		a	John Tobin,	John Bagwell, Esq.	House, office, and yard,	—	—	0 19 0	0 19
–		b	John Power,	John Bagwell, Esq.	House, office, and gar.	0 0 19	0 1 0	1 9 0	1 10
3	A B C d D		James Cooney,	Earl of Donoughmore,	House, offices, & land,	63 2 17	53 17 0	5 0 0	58 17
–		b	Mary Griffin (Hanrahan),	James Cooney,	House and yard,	—	—	0 13 0	0 13
–	D	a	Vacant,	James Cooney,	House,	—	—	0 8 0	0 8
12	A a	B	Bridget Keily,	Earl of Donoughmore,	House, offices, & land,	13 0 11	8 5 0	5 3 0	13 8
13			Mary Griffin (Coghlan),	Earl of Donoughmore,	House, offices, & land,	0 2 38	0 12 0	1 6 0	1 18
14			Patrick Coghlan,	Earl of Donoughmore,	House and land,	6 0 2	3 5 0	0 18 0	4 3
15			Denis M'Enery,	Earl of Donoughmore,	Land,	6 2 4	3 11 0	—	3 11
16					River Suir,	8 3 18	—	—	
				Total,		710 3 24	364 5 0	32 6 0	396 11

Figure 37. Widow's Maiden Name

7. Although there is no other occupier of the same name in Figure 38, Bridget M'Mahon has "widow" appended to her name; Bridget O'Brien does not have this agnomen added to her name. The author contends that "widow" identifies the individual who is financially responsible for the taxes in a household of two adult women with the same name.

		KNOCKDOOCUNNA. (Ord. S. 35.)						
1		Felix Joseph M'Carthy,	Maurice O'Connell,	Land,	90 2 10	45 0 0	—	45 0 0
2	a	Patrick M'Namara,	Same,	House and land,	1 1 10	0 13 0	0 7 0	1 0 0
3	a	James Barron,	Same,	House, offices, and land,	22 2 10	12 0 0	0 15 0	12 15 0
4		Cornelius Halloran,	Same,	Land,	23 2 20	18 0 0	—	18 0 0
–	a	Bridget O'Brien,	Same,	House,	—	—	0 5 0	0 5 0
5	a	John Morony,	Same,	House, office, and land,	4 1 15	3 5 0	0 15 0	4 0 0
11	a	James M'Carthy,	Same,	House and garden,	0 0 20	0 2 0	0 3 0	0 5 0
12	a	Bridget M'Mahon(wid.),	Same,	House and land,	1 2 20	0 5 0	0 5 0	0 10 0
13			Earl of Kenmare,		10 0 10	7 5 0	—	
14		Maurice O'Connell	James John Baggott,	Land,	0 2 20	0 5 0	—	7 15 0
15			Rev. Ed.Jos.O'Reilly,		18 0 20	0 5 0	—	
				Total,	182 0 13	89 17 0	4 3 0	94 0 0

Figure 38. Widow

8. Anne Smyth, on the other hand, in figure 39 is listed as the **responsible occupier** of Holding No. 5b whose landlord is John Smyth of 5a. Her house valued at 15 shillings indicates a substantial building of stone walls with a slated roof. Is Anne a widowed sister-in-law of John Smyth? If Anne is John's widowed mother, might she not live in the same house with her son and daughter-in-law? If she is his widowed mother, why is she "renting" from her son? Perhaps, she is John's unmarried sister whose holding for a house was separated from the family farm of 32 acres when John married? Questions about this relationship would seem to suggest that death and marriage searches are in order.

		CROSSBANE. (Ord. S. 34 & 40.)						
1		Ultan Sullivan,	Reps. John Mayne,	House, offices, and land,	36 1 29	18 15 0	1 15 0	22 15
				Bog,	21 1 16	2 5 0	—	
2		Owen Monaghan,	Same,	House, office, and land,	8 0 15	3 0 0	0 10 0	3 10
3		Thomas Clarke,	Same,	House, offices, and land,	0 0 2	4 5 0	0 15 0	5 0
4		Jane Sullivan,	Same,	House, office, and land,	13 1 21	6 15 0	0 15 0	7 10
5	a	John Smyth,	Same,	House, offices, and land,	32 0 16	17 0 0	1 5 0	18 5
–	b	Anne Smyth,	John Smyth,	House,	—	—	0 15 0	0 15
6		Cornelius Sullivan,	Reps. John Mayne,	House, offices, and land,	25 0 28	13 10 0	1 0 0	14 10
7		Laurence Farrelly,	Same,	House, offices, and land,	18 1 18	9 5 0	1 0 0	10 5

Figure 39 Responsible Occupier

Unnamed Occupiers

The absence of an ancestor's name in a townland or in the entire civil parish does not necessarily indicate that he or she is dead, has moved to another area or emigrated. Other than the simple observation that an ancestor was not named as an occupier at the time the valuation was taken, possible explanations for his or her absence may be found.

1. Section 178 of the *Instructions* manual reads *"When a portion of a farm-house has been given up by a farmer to his father or mother, and no rent is paid for it to the farmer, or where a father or mother in giving up a farm to their son [or daughter] retains a portion of the house for his or her dwelling-house during his or her lifetime, such occupation does not form a distinct tenement."* Consequently, the parental name does not appear in the **Occupier** column.

No.		Occupier	Immediate Lessor	Description of Tenement	Area A. R. P.	Land £ s d	Buildings £ s d	Total £ s d
		MONEEN. (Ord. S. 27.)						
1		John Roche	James S. Greene, Esq.	House, office, and land	9 1 2	8 10 0	1 5 0	9 15 0
2	a	Peter Glasure	James S. Greene, Esq.	House, offices, and land	115 3 10	102 0 0	4 0 0	106 0 0
—	b	Ellen Roche	Peter Glazure	House	—	—	0 5 0	0 5 0
—	c	Catherine Tohill	Peter Glazure	House	—	—	0 5 0	0 5 0
—	d	Thomas Clancy, jun	Peter Glazure	House	—	—	0 8 0	0 8 0
—	e	Unoccupied	Peter Glazure	House	—	—	0 5 0	0 5 0
—	f	Jeremiah Howe	John Roche	House	—	—	0 5 0	0 5 0
—	g	Ellen Murphy	John Roche	House	—	—	0 5 0	0 5 0
—	h	Edward Murphy	John Roche	House and garden	0 0 38	0 5 0	0 5 0	0 10 0
—	i	William Cox	John Roche	House, offices, and gar.	0 1 16	0 8 0	0 12 0	1 0 0
—	j	John Thornhill	Peter Glazure	House, office, & garden	0 1 12	0 8 0	0 8 0	0 16 0
3	a	Martin Gallagher, sen.	James S. Greene, Esq.	Land	48 1 16	38 0 0	—	38 0 0
		Thomas Delane	Martin Gallaghar, sen.	House and garden	0 0 16	0 2 0	0 8 0	0 10 0
4 A a B		Thomas Barry	James S. Greene, Esq.	House, offices, and land	27 1 6	18 15 0	1 0 0	19 15 0
5		William Wilkinson	James S. Greene, Esq.	House and land	9 1 10	6 10 0	0 5 0	6 15 0
6		James S. Greene, Esq.	In fee	Land	32 2 9	24 0 0	—	24 0 0
—	a	Unoccupied	James S. Greene, Esq.	House and offices	—	—	1 0 0	1 0 0
7		Edward Higgins	James S. Greene, Esq.	House, offices, and land	16 1 10	10 15 0	1 0 0	11 15 0
8		Edward Finn	James S. Greene, Esq.	House, offices, and land	11 0 19	7 15 0	0 15 0	8 10 0
9	a	Thomas Nagle	James S. Greene, Esq.	House and land	5 3 24	4 0 0	0 10 0	4 10 0
—	b	Mary Quane	James S. Greene, Esq.	House and garden	0 0 15	0 2 0	0 6 0	0 8 0
—	c	Edward Brien	James S. Greene, Esq.	House and garden	0 0 27	0 2 0	0 8 0	0 10 0
				Total,	277 0 30	221 12 0	13 15 0	235 7 0

Figure 40. Junior Responsible Occupier

2. On occasion, as illustrated in figure 40, "Thomas Clancey jun." appears among the occupiers, but there is no similiar name in the townland signifying a "senior." The inclusion of the "junior" agnomen may indicate that there are indeed two adult men of the same name residing on the holding, a son who now pays the rent and taxes and a father who is "retired" from that responsibility. Similarly, a "Mary Lahey (senior)" in the Occupier Column may well indicate that she is the responsible taxpayer, even though there is another adult Mary Lahey in residence, a daughter or a daughter-in-law..

3. If one or more buildings such as "herd's, steward's house, porter's lodges, or gate houses" is part of a tenement as shown in figure 41, Section 177 of the *Instructions* requires that it be specifically listed in the **Description of Tenement** column. Burton Persse is owner of the 806+ acres in Holding #2 in Moyode, but it is unlikely that he resides in a herd's house valued at 15 shillings or even that of a cottier! Because this holding appears to be grazing land, it is likely that the two houses are occupied; but by whom? A search of Persse estate records may uncover their identity.

		MOYODE. (Ord. S. 96.)							
1		Patrick Noakley,	Burton Persse, .	House and land, .	1	3 30	0 15 0	0 10 0	1 5 0
2	a	Burton Persse, .	In fee, . .	{ Herd's house and land,	806	2 30	197 10 0	0 15 0	} 199 5 0
-	b			Cottier's house & office,	—		—	1 0 0	
3		Thomas Regan,	Burton Persse, .	House and land. .	2	3 6	1 0 0	2 0 0	3 0 0
4		Bartw. Molowney,	Same, .	House and land, .	2	0 35	0 15 0	0 15 0	1 10 0

Figure 41. Herd's House, Unnamed Occupier

4. Although it appears more frequently in towns and cities, the agnomen "lodger" is used in rural areas as well, figure 42. *"For any house let in separate apartments or lodgings, the immediate lessor is to be entered as the occupier with the observation lodger"* observes Section 34 of the *Instructions*.

		AGHNAHOLA. (Ord. S. 16.)							
1	a	Patrick Fitzpatrick, .	Lord Cremorne,	House,offices,and land,	69	1 15	87 10 0	10 0 0	77 10 0
-	b	Police barrack & yard,	(*See Exemptions.*)						
-	c	Patrick Fitzpatrick,	. . .	*Half annual rent,* .	—		—	—	7 0 0
-	c	Pk. Fitzpatrick (*lodgers*),	Patrick Fitzpatrick, .	House. . .	—		—	4 0 0	4 0 0
-	d	James M'Mahon, .	Same. . .	House. . .	—		—	0 10 0	0 10 0

Figure 42. Lodgers, Unnamed Occupiers

5. Another type of occupier as described in Section 34 of the *Instructions* is illustrated in Figures 43 and 44: *"When Tenements are let for a single crop, or for short periods, to a succession of persons ... the immediate lessor should, in such cases, be entered as the occupier ... ."*

		TERMON. (Ord. S. 33.)							
1	a	Michael Owens, .	Rev. Orange Kellett,	{ House,offices, and land,	24	0 23	10 3 0	0 10 0	} 10 15 0
				Bog, . . .	2	0 38	0 2 0	—	
-	b	Michl. Owens' labourer	Michael Owens, .	House, . .	—		—	0 5 0	0 5 0
2		Michael Owens, .	Rev. Orange Kellett, .	Land, . .	5	2 29	1 15 0	—	1 15 0
3		Nicholas Corny. .	Same, .	House,offices,and land,	31	0 24	12 5 0	1 0 0	13 5 0
4		} Patrick M'Mahon, sen.,	Same, .	{ House, office, and land,	9	0 25	3 0 0	0 10 0	} 4 5 0
5				Land, . .	1	1 4	0 15 0	—	
6		John Smith, . .	Same, .	House and land, .	9	0 22	4 5 0	0 10 0	4 15 0
7		Peter Lynch, . .	Same, .	House,offices,and land,	13	2 34	7 0 0	0 15 0	7 15 0
8		Thomas Tracey, .	Same, .	House,offices,and land,	12	1 9	4 0 0	0 10 0	4 10 0
9		Patrick Traynor, .	Same, .	{ House, office, and land,	14	0 33	5 13 0	0 10 0	} 6 5 0
				Bog, . . .	2	2 9	0 2 0	—	

Figure 43. Unnamed Labourer

	ASTAGOB							
1	Matthew Rice	Thomas Kannan Esq	Land	20 3 19	39 1 0	—	39 1 0	
2	Patrick Tuite	Thomas Kannan Esq	House, offices, and land	2 2 16	4 12 0	8 0 0	12 12 0	
3	Thomas M'Guire	Thomas Kannan Esq	House, iron foundry, offices, and garden	0 0 20	0 5 0	52 0 0	52 5 0	
			Waste under houses and roads	0 3 0	—	—	—	
4	Lucinda Wilson	Thomas Kannan Esq	House, offices and land	1 2 21	2 17 0	12 0 0	14 17 0	
5	Christopher Roe	Thomas Kannan Esq	House, office and land	1 1 12	2 9 0	2 8 0	4 17 0	
6	Michael Burke	Thomas Kannan Esq	House and land	0 3 0	1 8 0	1 18 0	3 6 0	
7	Matthew Purcell	Thomas Kannan Esq	House and land	0 3 6	1 10 0	1 18 0	3 8 0	
8	James Durneen or Cuffs	Heirs of Col Thos White	House, office and land	2 2 23	5 2 0	1 15 0	6 17 0	
9 a	Thomas Liddy	Thomas Kannan Esq	House, offices and land	8 1 27	21 18 0	16 0 0	37 18 0	
b	Thomas Liddy	Thomas Kannan Esq	House, paper manufactory	—	—	76 0 0	76 0 0	
c	Peter Moore	Thomas Liddy	House	—	—	3 15 0	3 15 0	
d	Thomas Liddy and others	Thomas Liddy	House	—	—	3 18 0	3 18 0	
e	Thomas Liddy and others	Thomas Liddy	House	—	—	4 0 0	4 0 0	
f	Thomas Liddy and others	Thomas Liddy	House	—	—	2 16 0	2 16 0	

Figure 44. Immediate Lessor with Unnamed Occupier

Legal Terms

There are legal terms and expressions found in the valuation that may aid in expanding information about an ancestor. They are found generally in the **Occupier** or **Immediate Lessor** columns.

1. The term *in fee* found in the **Immediate Lessor** column, by way of illustration, serves to identify the landowner of the tenement whose estate papers may contain information in a lease document, a rent book or other similar materials. A search for estate papers in *Manuscript Sources for the History of Irish Civilization* is appropriate.[94] Likewise, a listing under **Immediate Lessor** of a landlord who rents extensive property from the landowner and subsequently sublets it to tenants calls for a further search of this middleman's tenant records.

		BALLYLISHEEN. (Ord. S. 27.)						
1		Caleb Going, Esq.	In fee,	Land,	9 1 26	4 14 0	—	4 14 0
2 a		Commissioners of National Education,	Caleb Going. Esq.	School-house and yard,	—	—	3 10 0	3 10 0
— b		Patrick Kelly,	Caleb Going, Esq.	House and garden,	1 3 28	1 8 0	0 9 0	1 17 0
				Total,	11 1 14	6 2 0	3 19 0	10 1 0
				Exemptions: National School-house and yard,	—	—	3 10 0	3 10 0
				Total, exclusive of exemptions,	11 1 14	6 2 0	0 9 0	6 11 0

Figure 45. In Fee

---

[94] Richard J. Hayes, *Manuscript Sources for the History of Irish Civilisation* , 14 vols. (Boston: G.K. Hall & Co. 1965). FHL microfilm numbers 1440939 - 1440943.

2. *Reps of,* an abbreviation for "representatives of" indicates that the individual named in the valuation, Richard Hawkshaw, Esq., for example, in figure 46 was dead at the time it was taken, and his legal interest in the holding was being temporarily represented by a family member or perhaps by an executor named in a will. Among the duties of an executor are the responsibility to prove the will in court, to call in all debts owed to the deceased and to pay his or her outstanding debts, and to distribute legacies to those named in the will.[95] Each of these responsibilities suggests a paper trail to the deceased.

		BARNAGORE. (Ord. Ss. 27 & 33.)							
1	a	Philip Ryan,	Reps. of Richard Hawkshaw, Esq.	House, office, & land,			9 8 0	1 18 0	11 6 0
	b	Matthew Ryan,		House, office, & land,			9 8 0	1 15 0	11 3 0
	c	Michael Ryan,		House, office, & land,	133 2 2		12 14 0	1 5 0	13 19 0
	d	James Ryan,		House, office, & land,			18 15 0	1 13 0	20 8 0
	e	Patrick Ryan,		House, office, & land.			18 15 0	2 5 0	21 0 0
2		Philip Ryan, sen.	Michael Ryan,	House, office, and land.	10 2 29		6 2 0	0 16 0	6 18 0
3		Philip Ryan (Miller),	Representatives of Rcd. Hawkshaw, Esq.	House and land,	25 0 12		10 3 0	1 10 0	11 13 0
4	a	Michael Mara,	Representatives of Rd. Hawkshaw, Esq.	Ho., offices, and land,			11 6 0	1 11 0	12 17 0
–	b	John Renahan,		Ho., offices, and land,	50 3 7		5 13 0	0 17 0	6 10 0
–	c	Martin Mara,		Ho., offices, and land,			5 13 0	0 14 0	6 7 0
–	d	Patrick Renahan,	John Renahan,	House,	–		–	0 10 0	0 10 0
5		Michael Mara,	Representatives of Rcd. Hawkshaw, Esq.	Land,	3 1 16		1 4 0	–	1 4 0
6	A & B	Michael Roohan,	Representatives of Rcd.						

Figure 46. Representative of

3. The Court of Chancery served to settle disputes between parties by using rules of equity and conscience to give relief to the parties when no remedy was to be found by a strict interpretation of the law in a common-law court. The term *in Chancery* or *Court of Chancery* as shown in figure 47, will signal court documents that may well include genealogical information. If the term is used with the landowner or landlord of the townland, a search of the court documents may reveal information abouts the tenants in the townland.

The Court of Chancery was part of the " Four Courts" complex that was damaged in 1922.[96] However, some Chancery records predating this disaster did survive and are catalogued in several *Report of the Deputy Keeper*.[97]

		KILKIP, EAST. (Ord. S. 23.)							
1		John Carroll,	Court of Chancery.	Land,	5 2 23	4 0 0	–	4 0
–	a	Margaret Phelan,	John Carroll,	House and garden,	0 0 12	0 2 0	0 5 0	0 7
–	b	John Phelan,	John Carroll,	House,	–	–	0 5 0	0 5
–	c	John Devitt,	John Carroll,	House,	–	–	0 5 0	0 5
2	a	Thomas Carroll,	Court of Chancery,	House and land,	2 0 28	2 0 0	0 10 0	2 10
–	b	Edward Fogarty,	Thomas Carroll,	House & small garden,	–	–	0 10 0	0 10
3		Patk. Keshan (of the Glen)	Court of Chancery,	Land,	7 1 25	7 5 0	–	7 5
–	a	Michael Motan,	Patrick Keshan,	House and garden,	0 1 6	0 5 0	1 0 0	1 5
4		John Kennedy,	Court of Chancery,	House, offices, and land,	20 2 33	16 0 0	1 0 0	17 0

Figure 47. Court of Chancery

---

[95] J.A. Strahan, *General View of the Law of Property*, (London: Stevens and Sons, Limited, 1926).

[96] The Courts Complex included the Exchequer, King's Bench, Chancery and Common Pleas.

[97] *Fifty-Fifth Report of the Deputy Keeper* - *Fifty-Eight Report of the Deputy Keeper*, (Dublin: Stationary Office, 1949 - 1951).

4. **Free** is an infrequent but curious term found in rural and urban listings of the valuation. Section 41 of the *Instructions* manual states that *"persons who hold by right of possession, and recognize no landlord, their tenure shall be entered as free."* Such an occupier whose holding is usually only a house might be termed a "squatter." In the case of Mary Lacey in figure 48 we note that her house is part of Holding No. 33 along with a Patrick Sweeney and a Peter Sweeney in the townland of Cloonkeen, Co. Roscommon. Patrick Sweeney is by far the largest occupier in the townland whose 47 holdings cover 1181+ acres. Is there a family relationship among these three persons? Are they father, son and widowed daughter? Are they brothers and a widowed sister? Is Mary Lacey a maiden name?

Notice the £12 taxable value of Patrick Sweeney's house and offices as compared to the Peter Sweeney and Mary Lacey houses at 5 shillings each. Who pays the taxes on her house? Failure to pay taxes could lead to ejectment by her immediate landlord Patrick Sweeney if not by the landowner William R. W. Sanford from whom Sweeney rents his own 161 acres.

Mary Lacey is the only "free" occupier in the area.

Figure 48. Free

4. **Freeholder** is an infrequent term found in the Immediate Lessor column. Section 37 of the Instructions states that *"The tenure of the rector or incumbent of a [Church of Ireland] parish in the cases of church or glebe lands, should be described as 'freehold.'"*

Figure 49. Freehold

The Purchase of Land

In 1870 the Land and Tenant Act (Ireland) was enacted by Parliament. Under the provisions of this Act *"the landlords and tenants of agricultural or pastoral holdings could arrange for advanced by the Board of Works, to be repaid ... by an annuity... ."*[98]

Although some prosperous tenants did take advantage of the Act, it was not until the passage of the Land Act of 1891 that the small and medium farmer was enabled to purchase his holding. The government advanced the total purchase money which was to be repaid over a forty-nine year period at an interest rate of 4%.

Figure 50 illustrates the Index page to a Revision Book in which the first notice is given that holdings within the book with the letters L A P (Land Act Purchase) have been purchased under the terms of the Act.

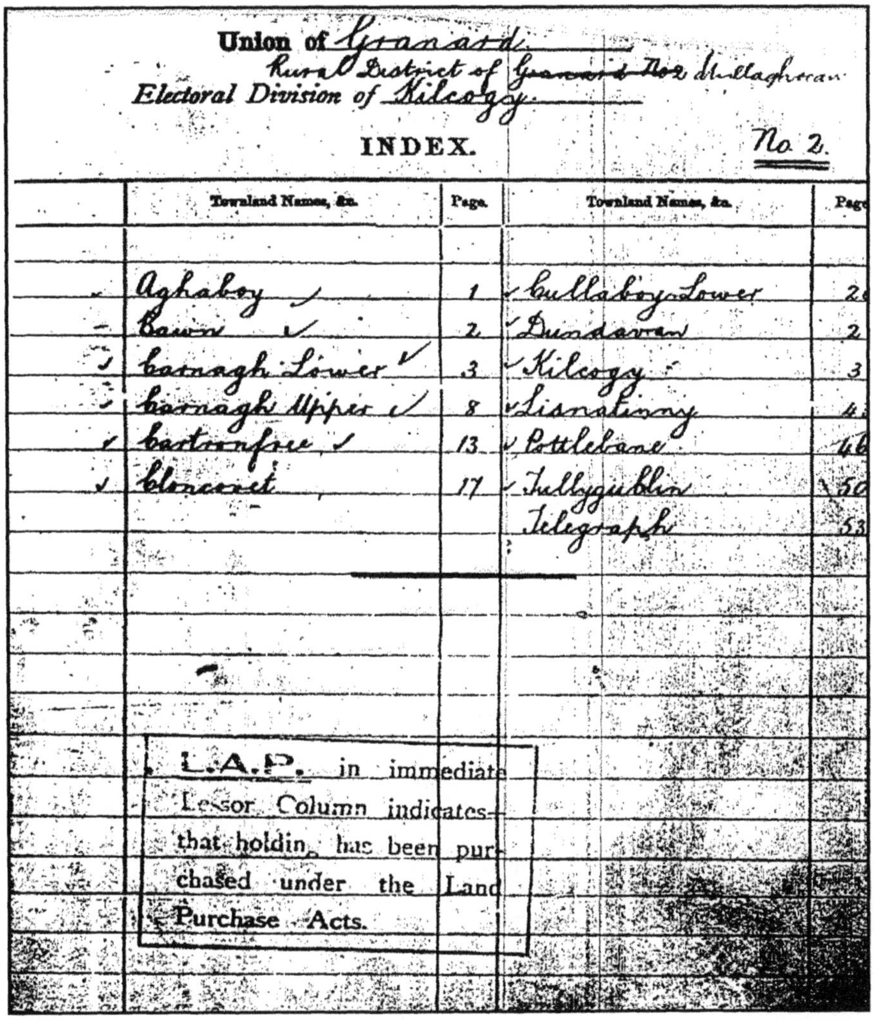

Figure 50. Land Act Purchase Designation

---

[98] Ernest F. Leet and R.R. McCutcheon, *A Sketch of The Law of Property in Ireland.* Dublin: Hodges, Figgis & Co., 1937, p. 30 - 31.

Figure 51 is a copy of the Registration of Title filed in the Registry of Deeds for the purchase on October 31, 1892 by the author's great grandfather of the ancestral holding of nine acres, one rood and sixteen perches in the townland of Pottlebane, parish of Drumlumman, Co. Cavan.

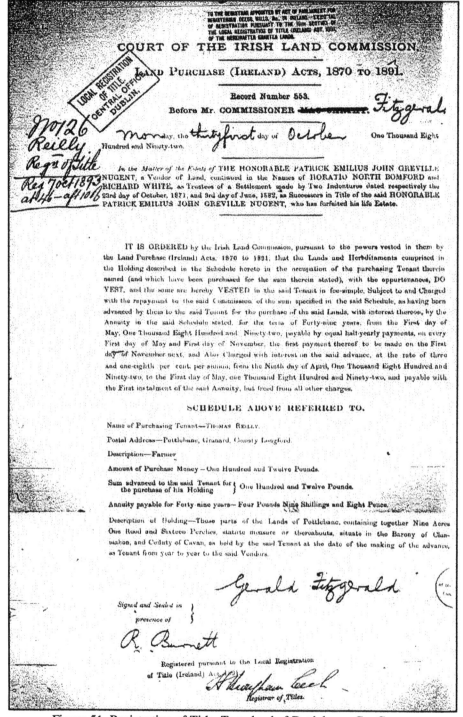

Figure 51. Registration of Title, Townland of Pottlebane, Co. Cavan.
Registry of Deeds

Appendix No. 1

Glossary

Acreage. Griffith measured land in the Valuation by <u>statute</u> acre, rood and perch; a statute acre contained 4840 square yards regardless of its shape; a rood was one-quarter of an acre of 1210 square yards; a perche was one fortieth of a rood containing thirty square yards.

Applotter. A person experienced in valuing property, both land and buildings.

Applotment. That share of the total tax that was imposed upon each individual responsible to pay taxes.

Barony. Historically based on original Gaelic family territory by the Anglo-Norman occupiers. 273 in number, their boundaries can cross county and civil parish lines.

Civil parish. Together with the townland the civil parish is a key administrative division of land for the researcher. Based on early medieval monastic and church settlements, its boundaries essentially reflect the area covered by the ecclesiastical parishes of the Protestant Church of Ireland. Roman Catholic parishes are infrequently coterminous with them. "Parish" in research customarily means civil not church parish. Numbering 2508 (Mitchell, *A New Genealogical Atlas of Ireland*, 1986), they frequently cross both barony and county borders. Occasionally a civil parish is divided into several separate parts!

Cottier/labourer. A landless person renting and cultivating a small holding under a system called cottier tenure. The main feature of this system was the letting of the land annually in small portions directly to labourers, the rent being fixed not by private agreement but by public competition. Oxford English Dictionary, Clarendon Press, Oxford, 1933.

County. A major land division created for local governmental purposes by the English between the Norman invasion and 1606. There are thirty-two counties, six in Northern Ireland and twenty-six in the Republic of Ireland.

County Cess. A local tax levied on the occupiers of land (owner and tenant) to finance the operation of the grand jury.

Grand Jury. A body of twenty three of the of the largest landholders in a county selected by the high sheriff in the spring and summer to meet with the crown's circuit judges to present indictments for criminal charges and to serve as the financial body to impose the taxes for the repair of roads and bridges, the erection of courthouses and jails.

Immediate Lessor. The landowner who occupies a property; or the middleman who leases from the landowner and in turn rents all or part of the property to another individual. Landowner and middleman are customarily referred to as landlords.

Lease. The term of a lease was frequently twenty-one years (a lease of years). More often its length was set by the number of years remaining in the lives of three named individuals (a lease of lives) agreed upon by the landlord and tenant. Although not required, the three lives usually included the lessee, his youngest child and a third person. The lease remained in force and the rent agreement unchanged until the death of the last named person. It was not unheard of for the third person to be the reigning monarch or a royal child whose death was easily confirmed.

Lot. A section of land with a single physical quality.

Middleman. An individual who leases a sizeable quantity of land from a landower and, in turn, sublets it to tenants, often at an excessive rent (rack rent).

Occupier. The individual or corporation who owns, leases or rents a tenement, commonly called a holding, and is financially responsible for the taxes levied on the tenement.

Plantation. A section of an estate set aside by its owner for the planting and cultivation of ornamental trees and shrubbery for planting on his manse.

Quality lot. The parts of a holding distinguished by the quality of the soil for valuation purposes.

Rural District. An administrative division created by the Local Government (Ireland) Act, 1898 when the the Poor Law Unions were dismantled. Its boundaries were the same as the original poor law union electoral divisions.

Shilling. In mid-nineteenth century Ireland twelve pence (d) equaled one shilling (s) twenty shillings equaled one pound (£). For example, £10-11s-3d + £2 -10s - 11d = £13-2s-2d

Tenant. An individual who rents or leases a property by the payment of a stated rent from a middleman or owner.

Tenement. Under the Act 15 & 16 Vic., c. 63 (Valuation of Rateable Property Act) a tenement is any taxable property (building structure and land) that is held or possessed for any time period (term), whether owned, leased, rented (tenure) for not less than year to year. One person may hold several distinct tenements and several persons may hold one tenement. *Instructions to Valuators and Surveyors, 1852.*

Townland. The smallest of the governmental administrative land districts, it frequently take its name from physical characteristics of the area such as ruins of churches and forts, and clan and family surnames.

Appendix No. 2

Ordnance Survey Memoirs published by The Institute of Irish Studies,
The Queen's University of Belfast, 1990 - 1998

Parishes of

Volume 1.   Co. Armagh, Parishes of Co. Armagh, 1835-1838
Volume 2   Co. Antrim I, 1838-9: Ballymartin, Ballyrobert,Ballywalter,Carnmoney,
             Mullusk
Volume 3.   Co. Down I, 1834-6: South Down
Volume 4.   Co. Fermanagh I, 1834-5: Enniskillen and Upper Lough Erne
Volume 5.   Co. Tyrone I, 1821, 1823, 1831-6: North, West and South Tyrone
Volume 6.   Co. Londonderry I, 1830, 1834, 1836: Arboe, Artrea, Ballinderry, Bal
             lyscullion, Magherafelt,   and Termoneeny
Volume 7.   Co. Down II, 1832-4, 1837: North Down and The Ards
Volume 8.   Co. Antrim II, 1832-8: Lisburn and South Antrim
Volume 9.   Co. Londonderry II, 1833-5: Roe Valley Central
Volume 10.   Co. Antrim III, 1833, 1835, 1839-40: Larne and Island Magee
Volume 11.   Co. Londonderry III, 1831-5: Roe Valley Lower
Volume 12.   Co. Down III, 1833-8: Mid-Down
Volume 13.   Co. Antrim IV, 1830-8: Glens of Antrim
Volume 14.   Co. Fermanagh II, 1834-5: Lower Lough Erne
Volume 15.   Co. Londonderry IV, 1824, 1833-5: Roe Valley Upper-Dungiven
Volume 16.   Co. Antrim V, 1830-5, 1837-8: Giant's Causeway and Balleymoney
Volume 17.   Co. Down IV, 1833-7: East Down and Lecale
Volume 18.   Co. Londonderry V, 1830, 1833, 1836-7: Maghera and Tamlaght O'Cuilly
Volume 19.   Co. Antrim VI, 1830, 1833, 1836-7: South-West Antrim
Volume 20.   Co. Tyrone II, 1825, 1833-5, 1840: Mid and East Tyrone
Volume 21.   Co. Antrim VII, 1832-8:South Antrim
Volume 22.   Co. Londonderry VI, 1831, 1833, 1835-6: North-East Londonderry
Volume 23.   Co. Antrim VIII, 1831-5, 1837-8: Ballymena and West Antrim
Volume 24.   Co. Antrim IX, 1830-2, 1835, 1838-9
Volume 25.   Co. Londonderry VII, 1834-5: North-West Londonderry
Volume 26.   Co, Antrim X, 1830-1, 1833-5, 1839-40: East Antrim, Glynn, Kilroot and
             Templecorran
Volume 27.   Co. Londonderry VIII, 1830, 1833-7, 1839: East Londonderry
Volume 28,   Co. Londonderry IX, 1832-8: West Londonderry
Volume 29.   Co. Antrim IX, 1832-3, 1835-9: Antrim Town and Ballyclare
Volume 30.   Co. Londonderry X, 1833-5, 1838: Mid-Londonderry
Volume 31.   Co. Londonderry XI, 1821, 1833, 1836-7: South Londonderry
Volume 32.   Co. Antrim XII, 1832-3, 1835-40: Ballynure and district
Volume 33.   Co. Londonderry XII, 1829-30, 1832, 1834-6: Coleraine and Mouth of the
             Bann
Volume 34.   Co. Londonderry XIII, 1831-8: Clondermot and the Waterside
Volume 35.   Co. Antrim XIII, 1833, 1835, 1838: Templepatrick and district
Volume 36.   Co. Londonderry XIV, 1833-4, 1836, 1838: Faughanvale
Volume 37.   Co. Antrim XIV, 1832, 1839-40: Carrickfergus
Volume 38.   Co. Donegal I, 1833-5: North-East Donegal
Volume 39.   Co. Donegal II, 1835-36" Mid, West and South Donegal
Volume 40.   South Ulster 1834-8: Cavan, Leitrim, Louth, Monaghan and Sligo

Appendix No. 3.

Townland Valuation Field Books Containing Lot Occupier Names

Co. Carlow:	All parishes except Moyacomb and Barragh.
Co. Cavan:	Parish of Tomregan, townland of Agharaskelly.
Co. Clare:	Kilnasoolagh parish, townlands of Ballysallagh East and Ballynacragga.
Co. Cork:	All parishes.
Co. Dublin:	All parishes.
Co. Kerry:	All parishes.
Co. Kildare:	Parishes of Cloncurry, Donadea, Kilcock, Mainham.
Co. Kings:	Parishes of Aghancon, Barr, Clonmacnoise, Corbally, Ettagh, Gallen, Kilcolman, Killagall,(Wheery), Kinnitty, Lemanaghan, Letterluna, Reynagh, Roscomroe, Roscrea, Seirkieran, Tisaran.
Co. Laioghis:	Parishes of Abbeyleix, Aghaboe, Ballyadams, Borris, Clonenagh and Clonagheen, Curraclone, Donaghmore, Dysertenos, Erke, Fossy (Timahoe), Kilcolemanbane, Kilteale, Kyle, Mayanna, Offerlease, Rathdowney, Rathsaran, Skirk, Strabone, Stradbally, Timogue, Tullomy.
Co. Limerick:	All parishes.
Co. Longford:	Parishes of Abbeyschrule, Agharra, Ardagh, Ballymacormick, Forgney, Kilcommock, Killashee, Kilglass, Noughaval Taghasheenod, Taghshinny.
Co. Mayo:	Parishes of Ardagh, Ballynahaglish, Ballysakeery, Castlemore, Doonfeeny, Kilbride, Kilcolman, Kilfian, Kilmoremoy, Lackan, Rathreagh, Templemurry.
Co. Meath:	Parish of Dunboyne, Kilbride, Rathkenny.
Co. Roscommon:	Parishes of Castlemore, Tachmaconnell.
Co. Sligo:	Parishes of St. John's, Cloonoghil, Kilglass, Skreen
Co. Tipperary:	Kilfeacle, Inch, Bourney, Killoskehan, Doon, Kilsheelan, Rochestown, Clonoulty, Rathkennan, Horeabbey, Kilbarron, Kilkeary, Kilcomenty and Stradbally, Lickfin
Co. Waterford:	Lismore and Mocollop, Clashmore, Kilgobnet, Killea, Kilronan, Kilburn, Killaloah
Co. Westmeath:	All parishes except Killucan, Kilbride, Kilmacnevan, Russagh, Dysart, Piercetown, Templepatrick

Co. Wexford: All parishes except Kiltrisk, Doonooney, Killann, Kerloge, St. John's, Donnghmore, Ferne, Whitechurch Glynn

Co. Wicklow: All parishes except Calary, Derryglossary, Drumkay, Glenealy, Kil common, Kilcoole, Killiskey, Bray, Delganny, Kilmacanoge, Powerscourt, Crosspatrick, Kilbride, Donaghmore, Dunlavin, Frey-nostown, Kilranelagh, Rathbran, Rathsallagh, Rathcoole, Tober.

Appendix No. 4.

Administrative Divisions

Barony. The basic territorial division of Celtic Ireland was the *tuath* (the territorial holdings of a clan). Historically there was a resemblance between the name of the territorial holding (barony) and the clan name (tuath). From the sixteenth century onward the barony was widely used as an administrative, tax, and regional entity within the county. The barony ceased to be a territorial division at the end of the nineteenth century. There were 331 baronies in Ireland.

County. The thirty-two counties are a result of the imposition of the English shire system beginning in the 12th century. Shires were instruments of local government administered by sheriffs. These officials oversaw a great variety of functions including courts, collection of taxes, and maintenance of highways. These functions were a reason for fixing definitive boundaries.

Diocese. The Church of Ireland and the Irish Roman Catholic Church are divided into large territorial units known as dioceses that are composed of a number of ecclesiastical parishes. Diocesan boundaries do not correspond to county boundaries, nor do those of the two Churches correspond to each other.

Parish. In origin the parish is an ecclesiastical administrative division of great antiquity and indicates the area over which a clergyman exercised spiritual jurisdiction. With the extension of the Reformation to Ireland in the sixteenth century the parish ceased its prominence as a center of Catholic religious practice; it became a new civil territorial division as well as the ecclesiastical parish of the Established Church. The Catholic Church, deprived of its buildings and land, had to adapt itself to a new parochial system of church parishes that were large and unwieldy. Civil parishes frequently cross both barony and county boundaries. Catholic parishes, on the other hand, faithfully observe the county boundaries but often cross civil parish lines.

Poor Law Union. The 1838 Poor Relief Act divided the country into districts, "unions of townlands", in which the local tax-payers were to be financially responsible for the care of the poor in their area. Centered on a large market town each Union's boundaries often crossed county boundaries; the market town also served as the site of the Work House. Beginning in 1851 the Union was subdivided into dispensary districts generally supervised by a medical doctor.

Probate District. In 1858 a principal registry in Dublin and eleven district registries were established to prove wills and grant letters of administration. The boundaries of probate districts follow either county or barony divisions.

Province. The four provinces of modern Ireland - Ulster in the north, Leinster in the east, Munster in the south and Connaught in the west - form the largest units of geographical reference. The country was first divided into four provinces at the Synod of Kells in 1152 when the four Archdioceses of Armagh, Cashel, Tuam and Dublin were formed. In modern times the province is usually thought of as a cartographic and census division.

Superintendent Registrar's District. With the passage of the Civil Registration Act of 1863 each Poor Law Union also became known as a Superintendent Registrar's District for the registration of births, marriages and deaths; and each dispensary district served as a local registrar's district with the medical doctor generally serving as registrar. The boundaries of the new districts were coterminous with those of the Poor Law Union and the dispensary districts.

Townland. These are small areas of land such as family farms or a group of farms. The townland is the smallest of the administrative divisions. The average townland size is 350 acres - the smallest townland is a little over an acre while the largest is over 7,000 acres. Townlands frequently take their name from physical characteristics of the area, from ruins of churches or forts, and from clan names.

Appendix No. 5

Dates of Published Townland Valuations

"Published" refers to the date the printed townland valuation was released by the Valuation Office to the County Treasurer for setting the Grand Jury cess. Dates were extracted by the author from the published volumes of the Townland Valuation in the National Library of Ireland.

ULSTER
Londonderry 1836
Tyrone 1837
Antrim 1839
Down 1839
Donegal 1840
Fermanagh 1840
Monaghan 1840
Cavan 1841

LEINSTER
Louth 1840
Meath 1840
Longford 1843
Westmeath 1843
Wicklow 1843
Carlow 1844
Kildare 1844
Queens 1846
Kings 1846-1847
Kilkenny 1848
Wexford 1848

CONNAUGHT
Leitrim 1841-1842
Roscommon 1841-1842
Sligo 1843
Mayo 1844
Galway 1846

MUNSTER
Clare 1847

Appendix No. 6

Tenement Valuation: Commencement and Completion Dates 1846-1864[1]

Antrim 1860-1862
Carlow 1851-1853
Cavan 1855-1857
Clare 1854-1856
Cork 1848-1853
Donegal 1856-1858

Down 1862-1864
Dublin 1847-1853
Fermanagh 1861-1863
Galway 1855-1857
Kerry 1848-1853
Kildare 1852-1854
Kilkenny 1851-1853
Laois 1851-1853
Leitrim 1855-1857
Limerick 1848-1853
Londonderry 1857-1859
Longford 1853-1855
Louth 1853-1855
Mayo 1855-1857
Meath 1853-1855
Monaghan 1859-1861
Offaly 1853-1855
Roscommon 1856-1858
Sligo 1856-1858
Tipperary 1848-1853
Tyrone 1858-1860
Waterford 1848-1853
Westmeath 1853-1855
Wexford 1852-1854
Wicklow 1852-1854
Armagh 1863-1864

---

[1] F.W. Bailey. "The Government Valuation of Ireland". *Journal of the Statistical and Social Inquiry Society of Ireland*, Vol IX, 1893.

Appendix No. 7

Issue Dates of Unions for Rating Purposes

This is the date on which a union, or a portion of that union extending into another county, was issued by the Valuation Office to the Board of Guardians for the setting of its poor rates.

Abbeyleix*	30 January 1852	Clonakilty	9 June 1853
Antrim	13 June 1862	Clones	18 April 1863
Ardee	11 July 1854	Clonmel	3 May 1852
Armagh	23 May 1865	Coleraine	29 September1859
Athlone	28 June 1856	Cookstown	17 July 1860
Athy	12 February 1853	Cootehill	30 August 1858
Bailieborougth	9 June 1857	Cork	8 October 1853
Ballina	4 July 1857	Corofin	25 September1855
Ballinasloe	25 June 1857	Croom	24 January 1853
Ballinrobe	31 October 1857	Delvin	6 December 1854
Ballycastle	5 June 1862	Dingle	12 February 1853
Ballymahon	25 July 1855	Donaghmore*	3 February 1852
Ballymena	1 May 1862	Donegal	14 June 1858
Ballymoney	17 April 1862	Downpatrick	24 March 1864
Ballyshannon	3 June 1863	Drogheda	4 August 1854
Ballyvaughan	15 May 1856	Dromore, West	9 February 1858
Balrothery*	10 October 1850	Dublin, North*	14 October 1851
Baltinglass	7 August 1854	Dublin, South*	12 January 1851
Banbridge	7 July 1864	Dundalk	13 November1854
Bandon	6 April 1853	Dunfanaghy	22 April 1858
Bantry	23 January 1854	Dungannon	20 July 1860
Bawnboy	23 July 1857	Dungarvan*	8 September 1852
Belfast	11 March 1862	Dunmanway	16 August 1853
Belmullet	17 December 1855	Dunshaughlin	9 May 1854
Borrisokane	25 January 1853	Edenderry	15 August 1854
Boyle	7 September 1858	Ennis	2 July 1856
Cahirsiveen	23 April 1853	Enniscorthy	9 March 1854
Callan	16 April 1853	Enniskillen	6 July 1863
Carlow	14 February 1853	Ennistymon	15 July 1856
Carrickmacross	22 June 1861	Fermoy	21 September1853
Carrick-on-Shannon	29 July 1858	Galway	6 June 1856
Carrick-on-Suir*	19 May 1852	Glennamaddy	23 October 1856
Cashel*	17 May 1852	Glenties	29 April 1858
Castlebar	4 November 1857	Glin	18 February 1853
Castleblayney	2 March 1865	Gorey	22 October 1853
Castlecomer	11 October 1850	Gort	15 May 1856
Castlederg	21 March 1860	Gortin	14 April 1860
Castlerea	19 December 1857	Granard	3 May 1856
Castletown	27 May 1853	Inishowen	28 April 1858
Cavan	22 July 1857	Irvinestown	2 June 1863
Celbridge*	6 June 1851	Kanturk	16 May 1853
Claremorris	22 July 1857	Kells	11 April 1855
Clifden	22 December 1855	Kenmare	20 April 1853
Clogheen	16 April 1853	Kilkeel	31 March 1864
Clogher	16 June 1860	Kilkenny	29 January 1853

Killadysart	18 July 1855	Newry	3 January 1865
Killala	19 November1856	Nerwtownards	12 February 1864
Killarney	10 December 1853	Newtownlimavaddy 1 November1858	
Kilmacthomas*	17 August 1852	Oldcastle	10 November1856
Kilmallock	25 April 1853	Omagh	5 July 1860
Kilrush	28 June 1856	Oughterard	14 July 1855
Kinsale*	26 August 1852	Parsonstown	25 July 1855
Larne	13 June 1862	Portumna	29 April 1857
Letterkenny	8 July 1858	Rathdown*	5 July 1852
Limerick	15 January 1853	Rathdrum	31 August 1854
Lisburn	25 November1863	Rathkeale	4 April 1853
Lismore*	17 July 1852	Roscommon	31 October 1857
Lisnaskea	18 April 1863	Roscrea*	22 January 1852
Listowel	27 January 1853	Scarriff	5 July 1856
Londonderry	28 July 1858	Shillelagh	25 May 1854
Longford	1 August 1855	Skibbereen	21 January 1854
Loughrea	13 May 1857	Skull	23 January 1854
Lurgan	27 October 1864	Sligo	3 July 1858
Macroom	16 August 1853	Straband	30 June 1859
Magherafelt	12 July 1859	Stranorlar	6 July 1858
Mallow	13 June 1853	Strokestown	1 April 1858
Manorhamilton	29 October 1857	Swinford	10 July 1857
Middleton	12 November1853	Thomastown*	28 July 1852
Milford	28 July 1858	Thurles	1 July 1853
Mill-street	16 August 1853	Tipperary*	24 December 1852
Mitchellstown	30 April 1853	Tobercurry	25 May 1858
Mohill	29 August 1857	Tralee	2 December 1853
Monaghan	1 July 1861	Trim	30 April 1855
Mount Bellew	15 May 1856	Tuam	24 April 1857
Mountmellick*	6 April 1852	Tulla	5 July 1856
Mullingar	17 July 1855	Tullamore	7 March 1855
Naas	21 March 1854	Urlingford*	29 March 1852
Navan	5 April 1855	Waterford*	12 July 1852
Nenagh	1 April 1855	Westport	8 October 1855
Newcastle	9 April 1853	Wexford	29 September 1853
Newport	10 October 1855	Youghal	10 November 1853
New Ross	15 August 1853		

Appendix No. 8

Completion Dates of Counties under 15 & 16 Vict., Cap. 63

Carlow 28 June 1853
Cork 20 July 1853
Cork City 9 July 1853
Dublin 5 May 1853
Kerry 19 July 1853
Limerick 29 June 1853
Queens 28 June 1853
Tipperary 29 June 1853
Waterford 5 July 1853

Dublin City 31 Oct 1854
Kildare 18 July 1854
Wexford 7 July 1854
Wicklow 4 July 1854

Kings 2 July 1855
Longford 6 July 1855
Louth 5 July 1855
Meath 10 July 1855
Westmeath 5 July 1855

Clare 3 July 1856
Galway Town 14 July 1856
Cavan 25 June 1857
Galway 29 June 1857
Leitrim 6 July 1857
Mayo 13 July 1857

Donegal 6 July 1858
Roscommon 1 July 1858
Sligo 7 July 1858
Londonderry 16 July 1859

Tyrone 13 July 1860

Monaghan 1 July 1861

Antrim 10 July 1862

Fermanagh 4 July 1863

Down 12 July 1864

Armagh 1 June 1865

Appendix No. 9

A INVENTORY OF THE BOOKS OF SIR RICHARD GRIFFITH'S GENERAL VALUATION OF RATEABLE PROPERTY IN IRELAND CONDUCTED UNDER 9 & 10 VICT., C. 110 1846 AND 15 & 16 VICT., C. 63, 1852

1. Part 1 of the Inventory is an alphabetical listing by county of the poor law union holdings of each repository. Part 2 is a full alphabetical listing by poor law union of the holdings of all repositories.

2. Column Headings:

Repository: its number, as noted at the foot of each inventory page, indicates that a copy of the valuation is in its holdings; a "0" indicates no copy in its collection. "CL" means that a copy of the valuation is in the appropriate county library.

Printing Date: Valuation Office date of printing as it appears on the title page of the printed or manuscript book.

Act: Act of Parliament under which the valuation was performed.

Film: microfilm number [item on film] of the Valuation in the Family History Library, Salt Lake City.

Vol: the printed volume of the Valuation in the Family History Library collection.

Remarks: notations of variations in arrangement, content, and style of publication added by the compiler.

3. Notes:

Alterations Only: a revised and amended Valuation listing only occupiers whose holdings were mofified.

Electoral Division: Valuation is indexed by poor law union electoral division rather than by civil parish.

Manuscript: copy is in manuscript format.

"9&10A" indicates that a "Primary Valuation" has been revised and amended by the Sub-Commissioners of Valuation after appeals by rate-payers; dates of these altered books are not shown in the Select Committee listing of dates.

"Not Listed" indicates that the date of printing shown on the title page is not listed in the 1869 Committee Report

Parish with Electoral Division: Valuation is indexed by civil parish and electoral division.

Photocopy: Not an original copy of valuation.

Private Collection: Not found by compiler in the named repositories but in a private individual's library.

SC Date: printing date of the primary valuation of each union as submitted by the Commis sioner of Valuation to the Parliamentary Select Committee of 1869. There are some differences between the Valuation Office dates and the Select Committee dates noted in the Remarks column.

AN INVENTORY OF THE BOOKS OF SIR RICHARD GRIFFITH'S
GENERAL VALUATION OF RATEABLE PROPERTY IN IRELAND

County	Poor Law Union	Printing Date Act Remarks Film[Item]	Repository Volume
Antrim	Antrim	27 March 1862 15&16 258749 [2]	0 2 3 4 5 0 0 8 CL
Antrim	Ballycastle	03 October 1861 15&16 258749 [3]	0 2 3 4 5 0 0 8 CL
Antrim	Ballymena	23 January 1862 15&16 258749 [4]	0 2 3 4 6 0 0 8 CL
Antrim	Ballymoney (Part of)	18 Septemb 1861 15&16 258749 [5]	0 2 3 4 5 0 0 8 CL
Antrim	Belfast (Part of)	17 October 1861 15&16 258756 [3]	0 2 3 4 5 0 0 8 CL
Antrim	Belfast (Part of)	17 October 1861 15&16 258749 [6]	0 2 3 4 5 0 0 8 CL
Antrim	Coleraine (Part of)	17 August 1859 15&16 258750 [1]	0 2 3 4 0 0 0 8 CL
Antrim	Larne	11 December 1861 15&16 258750 [2]	0 2 3 4 5 0 0 8 CL
Antrim	Lisburn (Part of)	30 April 1862 15&16 258750 [3]	0 2 3 4 5 0 0 8 CL
Antrim	Lurgan (Part of)	03 May 1862 15&16 258750 [4]	0 2 3 4 5 0 0 8 CL

An Inventory of the Books of Sir Richard Griffith's General Valuation of Rateable Property in Ireland

County	Poor Law Union	Printing Date / Act / Remarks	Film[Item]	Repository / Volume
Antrim & Down	Belfast Municipal Borough	22 November 1860 15&16 Not in Antrim County Library.	258756 [2]	0 2 3 4 5 0 0 8
Armagh	Armagh (Part of)	01 December 1864 15&16	258750 [5]	0 2 3 4 5 0 0 8
Armagh	Banbridge (Part of)	10 December 1863 15&16	258750 [6]	0 2 3 4 5 0 0 8
Armagh	Castleblaney (Part of)	03 October 1864 15&16 Copy in Monaghan County Library	258751 [1]	0 2 3 4 0 0 0 8
Armagh	Lurgan (Part of)	21 July 1864 15&16	258751 [2]	0 2 3 4 5 0 0 8
Armagh	Newry (Part of)	29 August 1864 15&16	258751 [3]	0 2 3 4 5 0 0 8 CL
Armagh, Louth & Monaghan	Dundalk	20 April 1854 15&16	844991 [7]	1 2 3 4 5 6 0 8 CL 121
Carlow	Carlow	01 April 1852 9&10 Copy in Wexford County Library	101755 [2]	1 2 3 4 5 0 0 0 CL
Cavan	Baileborough	01 November 1856 15&16	844975 (1)	0 2 3 4 5 6 0 8 CL 001
Cavan	Bawnboy (Part of)	14 April 1857 15&16	844975 (2)	1 2 3 4 5 6 0 8 CL 002

AN INVENTORY OF THE BOOKS OF SIR RICHARD GRIFFITH'S
GENERAL VALUATION OF RATEABLE PROPERTY IN IRELAND

County	Poor Law Union	Printing Date Act Remarks Film[Item]	Repository Volume
Cavan	Cavan	14 February 1857 15&16 844975 (3)	1 2 3 4 5 6 0 8 CL 003
Cavan	Cootehill	25 March 1857 15&16 844975[4)	1 2 3 4 5 6 0 8 CL 004
Cavan	Enniskillen	30 March 1857 15&16 844975 (5)	1 2 3 4 5 6 0 8 CL 005
Cavan	Granard	04 December 1855 15&16 844975 (6)	1 2 3 4 5 6 0 8 CL 006
Cavan	Oldcastle	17 June 1856 15&16 844975 (7)	0 2 3 4 5 6 0 8 CL 007
Clare	Ballyvaghen	28 June 1855 15&16 844976 (1)	1 2 3 4 5 6 0 0 CL 008
Clare	Corrofin	10 March 1855 15&16 844976 (2)	1 2 3 4 5 6 0 0 CL 009
Clare	Ennis	15 Septemb 1855 15&16 844976 (3)	1 2 3 4 5 6 0 0 CL 010
Clare	Ennistimon	12 Septemb 1855 15&16 844976 (4)	1 2 3 4 5 6 0 0 CL 011
Clare	Killadysert	18 July 1855 15&16 844976 (5)	1 2 3 0 5 6 0 0 CL 012

1-Valuation Office 2-Irish Microforms 3-Family History Library 4-National Library of Ireland
5-National Archives 6-Genealogical Office 7-Dublin Gilbert Library 8-PRONI CL-County Library

AN INVENTORY OF THE BOOKS OF SIR RICHARD GRIFFITH'S
GENERAL VALUATION OF RATEABLE PROPERTY IN IRELAND

County	Poor Law Union	Printing Date Act Remarks Film[Item]	Repository Volume
Clare	Kilrush	20 August 1855 15&16 844976 (6)	1 2 3 0 5 6 0 0 CL 013
Clare	Limerick (Part of)	08 March 1852 9&10 844976 (7)	0 2 3 0 5 6 0 0 CL 014
Clare	Tulla	20 Septemb 1855 15&16 844976 (8)	1 2 3 0 5 6 0 0 CL 015
Clare & Galway	Scariff	21 November 1855 15&16 844983 (3) Not in Galway County Library	1 2 3 0 5 6 0 0 CL 062
Cork	Bandon	15 December 1851 9&10 844978 (7)	1 2 3 4 5 6 0 0 CL 029
Cork	Bandon and Kinsale	25 June 1851 9&10 844978 (6) SC Not listed	1 2 3 4 5 6 0 0 CL 028
Cork	Bandon, Bantry, Clonakilty, Dunmanway and Skibberen	01 May 1852 9&10 101753 [3] 2, 3, 4 manuscript	1 2 3 4 0 0 0 0 CL
Cork	Bandon, Clonakilty, Drunmanway and Kinsale	24 July 1851 9&10 844977 (7)	1 2 3 4 5 6 0 0 CL 022
Cork	Bandon, Cork and Macroom	23 October 1852 15&16 844978 (1) 2, 3, 4, 5 manuscript	1 2 3 4 5 6 0 0 CL 023
Cork	Bantry	01 April 1852 9&10 101753 [1] 2, 3, 4 manuscript. Not in County Library	1 2 3 4 0 0 0 0

AN INVENTORY OF THE BOOKS OF SIR RICHARD GRIFFITH'S
GENERAL VALUATION OF RATEABLE PROPERTY IN IRELAND

County	Poor Law Union	Printing Date Act Remarks Film[Item]	Repository Volume
Cork	Bantry and Castletown	04 June 1852 9&10 844977 [3] 2, 3, 5, 6 manuscript	1 2 3 4 5 6 0 0 CL
Cork	Bantry, Skull and Skibbereen	20 July 1853 15&16 844979 [4]	1 2 3 4 5 6 0 0 CL 034
Cork	Clonakilty	12 January 1852 9&10 844978 (3)	1 2 3 4 5 6 0 0 CL 025
Cork	Cork	14 July 1852 15&16 101753[4]	1 2 3 4 5 0 0 0 CL
Cork	Cork	00 November 1852 15&16 844977 (5) 2, 3, 4, 5, 6 manuscript	1 2 3 4 5 6 0 0 CL 020
Cork	Cork and Kinsale	30 December 1850 9&10 844978 (5)	1 2 3 4 5 6 0 0 CL 027
Cork	Cork, Fermoy and Middleton	02 April 1853 15&16 844977 (2)	1 2 3 4 5 6 0 0 CL 017
Cork	Dunmanway, Macroon and Millstreet	00 November 1852 15&16 844979 (2) 2, 3, 4, 5 manuscript. SC 30 November	1 2 3 4 5 6 0 0 CL 032
Cork	Fermoy	02 Septemb 1850 9&10A SC date is same as Altered Printing Date	0 0 0 4 5 0 0 0 CL
Cork	Fermoy and Middleton	15 March 1850 9&10 844978 (8) 5 photocopy	1 2 3 4 5 0 0 0 CL 030

1-Valuation Office 2-Irish Microforms 3-Family History Library 4-National Library of Ireland
5-National Archives 6-Genealogical Office 7-Dublin Gilbert Library 8-PRONI CL-County Library

AN INVENTORY OF THE BOOKS OF SIR RICHARD GRIFFITH'S
GENERAL VALUATION OF RATEABLE PROPERTY IN IRELAND

County	Poor Law Union	Printing Date Act Remarks	Film[Item]	Repository Volume
Cork	Fermoy and Mitchelstown	23 February 1852 9&10	844977 (4)	1 2 3 4 5 6 0 0 CL 019
Cork	Fermoy, Mallow and Mitchelstown	01 May 1851 9&10	844978 (2)	1 2 3 4 5 6 0 0 CL 024
Cork	Kanturk, Kilmallock and Mallow	20 June 1851 9&10	844979 [1]	1 2 3 4 0 6 0 0 CL 029
Cork	Kanturk (Part 1)	10 March 1852 9&10 Not in County Library.	101753 [5]	1 2 3 4 5 0 0 0
Cork	Kinsale	03 March 1851 9&10 4 manuscript. Not in County Library.	101753 [2]	1 2 3 4 5 0 0 0
Cork	Kinsale	10 March 1852 9&10 2, 3, 4, 5, 6 manuscript	844978 (8)	1 2 3 4 5 6 0 0 CL 030
Cork	Mallow and Cork	10 March 1851 9&10	844977 (1)	1 2 3 4 5 6 0 0 CL 016
Cork	Mallow (Part 2)	10 March 1852 9&10	844977 (6)	0 2 3 4 5 6 0 0 CL 021
Cork	Millstreet (Part 3)	10 March 1852 9&10	844977 [6]	0 2 3 4 5 6 0 0 CL 021
Cork	Skibbereen	21 March 1853 15&16	844979 (3)	1 2 3 4 5 6 0 0 CL 033

1-Valuation Office 2-Irish Microforms 3-Family History Library 4-National Library of Ireland
5-National Archives 6-Genealogical Office 7-Dublin Gilbert Library 8-PRONI CL-County Library

AN INVENTORY OF THE BOOKS OF SIR RICHARD GRIFFITH'S
GENERAL VALUATION OF RATEABLE PROPERTY IN IRELAND

County	Poor Law Union	Printing Date Act Remarks Film[Item]	Repository Volume
Cork	Youghal and Middletown	27 June 1853 15&16 844978 (4)	1 2 3 4 5 6 0 0 CL 026
Donegal	Ballyshannon	23 February 1858 15&16 844979 (5)	1 2 3 4 5 6 0 8 CL 035
Donegal	Donegal	28 November 1857 15&16 844979 (6) Electoral Division	1 2 3 4 5 6 0 8 CL 036
Donegal	Dunfanaghy	21 Septemb 1857 15&16 844979 (7) Electoral Division	1 2 3 4 5 6 0 8 CL 037
Donegal	Glenties	11 Septemb 1857 15&16 844980 (1) Electoral Division	0 2 3 4 5 0 0 8 CL 038
Donegal	Inishowen	01 October 1857 15&16 844980 (2) Electoral Division	1 2 3 4 5 6 0 8 CL 039
Donegal	Letterkenny	15 February 1858 15&16 844980 (3) Electoral Division	1 2 3 4 5 6 0 8 CL 040
Donegal	Millford	27 March 1858 15&16 844980 (4)	1 2 3 4 5 6 0 8 CL 041
Donegal	Strabane	22 March 1858 15&16 844980 (5)	1 2 3 4 5 6 0 8 CL 042
Donegal	Stranorlar	07 December 1857 15&16 844980 (6) Electoral Division	1 2 3 4 5 6 0 8 CL 043

1-Valuation Office 2-Irish Microforms 3-Family History Library 4-National Library of Ireland
5-National Archives 6-Genealogical Office 7-Dublin Gilbert Library 8-PRONI CL-County Library

An Inventory of the Books of Sir Richard Griffith's General Valuation of Rateable Property in Ireland

County	Poor Law Union	Printing Date Act Remarks	Film[Item]	Repository Volume
Donegal & Londonderry	Londonderry	26 January 1858 15&16		02045008
		Electoral Division. Not in Donegal CL.		
Down	Banbridge	10 December 1863 15&16	258751 [4]	02345008
Down	Belfast (Outside Municipal Boundary)	17 October 1861 15&16	258751 [5]	02345008
Down	Downpatrick	26 Septemb 1863 15&16	258752 [1]	02345008
Down	Kilkeel	12 October 1863 15&16	258752 [2]	02345008
Down	Lisburn (Part of)	10 August 1863 15&16	258752 [3]	02345008
Down	Lurgan (Part of)	09 May 1864 15&16	258752 [4]	02345008
Down	Newry (Part of)	18 April 1864 15&16	258752 [5]	02345008
Down	Newtown Ards	15 July 1863 15&16	258753 [1]	02345008
Dublin	Balrothery	25 Septemb 1852 15&16	844981 (3)	12345670 047

1-Valuation Office 2-Irish Microforms 3-Family History Library 4-National Library of Ireland
5-National Archives 6-Genealogical Office 7-Dublin Gilbert Library 8-PRONI CL-County Library

AN INVENTORY OF THE BOOKS OF SIR RICHARD GRIFFITH'S
GENERAL VALUATION OF RATEABLE PROPERTY IN IRELAND

County	Poor Law Union	Printing Date Act Remarks Film[Item]	Repository Volume
Dublin	Balrothery	01 July 1847 9&10	1 0 0 0 5 0 7 0
Dublin	Balrothery	17 November 1847 9&10 SC Not listed; Private Collection	0 0 0 0 0 0 0 0
Dublin	Balrothery	01 June 1848 9&10A 844981 (4)	1 2 3 4 5 0 0 0 048
Dublin	Balrothery and Dunsloughlin, [Barony of Baltothery West]	15 June 1847 9&10	0 0 0 4 5 0 0 0
Dublin	Balrothery and Dunsloughlin, [Barony of Baltothery West]	15 May 1848 9&10A 844981 [6]	0 2 3 4 5 6 7 0 050
Dublin	Celbridge	18 May 1850 9&10	0 0 0 4 5 0 0 0
Dublin	Celbridge	24 June 1849 9&10A	1 2 0 0 5 0 0 0
Dublin	Celbridge	20 May 1851 9&10A 844981 (5) Electoral Division	0 0 3 4 0 0 7 0 049
Dublin	Celbridge	01 April 1851 9&10A 844981 (4) Electoral Division	0 0 3 0 0 0 0 0 048
Dublin	Celbridge and South Dublin	13 November 1847 9&10	0 0 0 0 5 0 0 0

AN INVENTORY OF THE BOOKS OF SIR RICHARD GRIFFITH'S
GENERAL VALUATION OF RATEABLE PROPERTY IN IRELAND

County	Poor Law Union	Printing Date Act Remarks Film[Item]	Repository Volume
Dublin	Celbridge and South Dublin	16 August 1848 9&10A	00000070
Dublin	North Dublin	27 May 1854 15&16 844980 (7)	12345670 044
Dublin	North Dublin and Balrothery	20 July 1848 9&10 SC Not Listed	12045000
Dublin	North Dublin and Balrothery Barony of Coolock	15 March 1850 9&10A 101754 [2]	00305000
Dublin	North Dublin and Celbridge	03 1847 9&10	00340000 158
Dublin	North Dublin and Celbridge	20 August 1848 9&10A	00040000
Dublin	North Dublin and Celbridge	20 March 1849 9&10A	02045070
Dublin	South Dublin	16 February 1854 15&16 844981 (1)	12345670 045
Dublin	South Dublin	15 February 1850 9&10A 101754 [1]	12345070
Dublin	South Dublin and Rathdown	20 October 1847 9&10	00040000

1-Valuation Office 2-Irish Microforms 3-Family History Library 4-National Library of Ireland
5-National Archives 6-Genealogical Office 7-Dublin Gilbert Library 8-PRONI CL-County Library

AN INVENTORY OF THE BOOKS OF SIR RICHARD GRIFFITH'S
GENERAL VALUATION OF RATEABLE PROPERTY IN IRELAND

County	Poor Law Union	Printing Date Act Remarks Film[Item]	Repository Volume
Dublin	South Dublin and Rathdown	10 March 1849 9&10 SC Not Listed	1 2 0 4 5 0 0 0
Dublin	South Dublin and Rathdown	05 Septemb 1848 9&10A	0 0 0 4 0 0 0 0
Dublin	South Dublin and Rathdown	02 January 1849 9&10A 844981 (2)	1 2 3 4 5 0 0 0 046
Dublin	South Dublin, Rathdown and Celbridge	10 November 1847 9&10	0 0 0 4 5 6 0 0
Fermanagh	Ballyshannon (Part of)	01 July 1862 15&16 258753 [2]	0 2 3 4 5 0 0 8 CL
Fermanagh	Clones (Part of)	08 August 1862 15&16 258758 [3]	0 2 3 4 5 0 0 8 CL
Fermanagh	Enniskillen (Part of)	10 December 1862 15&16 258753 [4]	0 2 3 4 5 0 0 8 CL
Fermanagh	Irvinestown [Lowtherstow pre-1862]	05 November 1862 15&16 258753 [5]	0 2 3 4 5 0 0 8 CL
Fermanagh	Lisnaskea	10 October 1862 15&16 258753 [6]	0 2 3 4 5 0 0 8 CL
Galway	Ballinasloe	20 November 1856 15&16 844981 (7)	1 2 3 4 5 6 0 0 CL 051

An Inventory of the Books of Sir Richard Griffith's
General Valuation of Rateable Property in Ireland

County	Poor Law Union	Printing Date Act Remarks Film[Item]	Repository Volume
Galway	Galway	07 March 1855 15&16 844981 (8)	1 2 3 4 5 6 0 0 CL 052
Galway	Loughrea	10 June 1856 15&16 844982 (1)	1 2 3 4 5 6 0 0 CL 053
Galway	Mountbellow	21 August 1855 15&16 844982 (2)	1 2 3 4 5 0 0 0 CL 054
Galway	Portumna	02 June 1856 15&16 844982 (3)	1 2 3 4 5 6 0 0 CL 055
Galway	Tuam	10 December 1855 15&16 844982 (4)	1 2 3 4 5 6 0 0 CL 056
Galway & Clare	Gort	31 August 1855 15&16 844982 (7) Copy in Clare County Library	1 2 3 4 5 6 0 0 CL 059
Galway & Mayo	Clifden	31 March 1855 15&16 844982 (5) Not in Mayo County Library.	1 2 3 4 5 6 0 0 CL 057
Galway & Mayo	Oughterard	24 January 1855 15&16 844983 (1) Copy in Mayo County Library.	1 2 3 4 5 6 0 0 CL 060
Galway & Roscommon	Glenamaddy	28 April 1856 15&16 844982 (6) Copy in Roscommon County Library.	1 2 3 4 5 6 0 0 CL 061
Kerry	Cahersiveen and Killarney	20 May 1852 9&10 101754 [3] SC 28 May 1852; 2, 3, 4, 5 manuscript	1 2 3 4 5 0 0 0 CL

1-Valuation Office 2-Irish Microforms 3-Family History Library 4-National Library of Ireland
5-National Archives 6-Genealogical Office 7-Dublin Gilbert Library 8-PRONI CL-County Library

AN INVENTORY OF THE BOOKS OF SIR RICHARD GRIFFITH'S
GENERAL VALUATION OF RATEABLE PROPERTY IN IRELAND

County	Poor Law Union	Printing Date Act Remarks Film[Item]	Repository Volume
Kerry	Cahersiveen, Kenmare and Killarney	27 August 1852 15&16 844984 (2)	1 2 3 0 5 0 0 0 CL 068
Kerry	Dingle and Tralee	02 August 1852 15&16 844983 (5) 2, 3, 5 manuscript	1 2 3 0 5 0 0 0 CL 064
Kerry	Glin and Listowel	15 December 1851 9&10 844983 (7)	1 2 3 4 5 0 0 0 CL 066
Kerry	Kenmare and Cahersiveen	28 Septemb 1852 15&16 844984 (2) 2, 3, 5 manuscript	1 2 3 0 5 0 0 0 CL 068
Kerry	Kenmare and Killarney	23 August 1852 15&16 844983 (6)	1 2 3 0 5 0 0 0 CL 065
Kerry	Killarney	23 April 1853 15&16 844984 (1)	1 2 3 4 5 0 0 0 CL 067
Kerry	Listowel and Tralee	22 January 1852 9&10 844983 (4)	1 2 3 0 5 0 0 0 CL 063
Kerry	Tralee, Killarney and Dingle	01 March 1853 15&16 844984 (3)	1 2 3 4 5 0 0 0 CL 069
Kildare	Athy and Baltinglass	24 July 1852 15&16 101755 [1]	1 2 3 4 5 0 0 0 CL
Kildare	Celbridge	20 May 1850 9&10 844984 (4]	1 0 3 4 0 0 0 0 CL 070

1-Valuation Office 2-Irish Microforms 3-Family History Library 4-National Library of Ireland
5-National Archives 6-Genealogical Office 7-Dublin Gilbert Library 8-PRONI CL-County Library

AN INVENTORY OF THE BOOKS OF SIR RICHARD GRIFFITH'S
GENERAL VALUATION OF RATEABLE PROPERTY IN IRELAND

County	Poor Law Union	Printing Date Act Remarks	Film[Item]	Repository Volume
Kildare	Celbridge	25 Septemb 1850 9&10	844984 (6)	0 0 3 4 5 0 0 0 CL 072
Kildare	Celbridge	07 May 1850 9&10	844984 (6)	1 0 3 4 0 0 0 0 CL 072
Kildare	Celbridge	02 Septemb 1850 9&10A Not in County Library.		0 0 0 0 0 0 7 0
Kildare	Celbridge	31 May 1851 9&10A Not in County Library.		0 2 0 4 5 0 0 0
Kildare	Celbridge	25 March 1851 9&10A Not in County Library.		0 2 0 4 0 6 0 0
Kildare	Celbridge	10 March 1851 9&10A Not in County Library.		0 2 0 4 5 0 0 0
Kildare	Edenderry	14 October 1853 15&16	844984 (4)	1 2 3 4 5 6 0 0 CL 070
Kildare	Naas	14 Septemb 1853 15&16	844984 (5)	1 2 3 4 5 0 0 0 CL 071
Kilkenny	Callan	12 October 1849 9&10 5 photocopy		1 2 0 0 5 6 0 0 CL
Kilkenny	Callan	2 May 1850 9&10A Alterations only. Not in County Library.	844984 [7]	0 0 3 0 5 6 0 0 073

1-Valuation Office 2-Irish Microforms 3-Family History Library 4-National Library of Ireland
5-National Archives 6-Genealogical Office 7-Dublin Gilbert Library 8-PRONI   CL-County Library

**AN INVENTORY OF THE BOOKS OF SIR RICHARD GRIFFITH'S
GENERAL VALUATION OF RATEABLE PROPERTY IN IRELAND**

County	Poor Law Union	Printing Date Act Remarks Film[Item]	Repository Volume
Kilkenny	Callan and Carrick -on -Suir	03 April 1850 9&10	1 2 0 4 5 0 0 0 CL
Kilkenny	Callan, Carrick-on-Suir, Kilkenny, New Ross and Waterford	10 April 1850 9&10 101755 [4] 5 photocopy	1 2 0 4 5 0 0 0 CL
Kilkenny	Callan, Kilkenny and Thomastown	05 October 1850 9&10A 844985 (6) Electoral Division	0 0 3 4 5 0 0 0 CL 078
Kilkenny	Callan, Kilkenny and Urlingford	12 Septemb 1850 9&10A 844984 (7) Not in County Library.	0 0 3 0 5 6 0 0 073
Kilkenny	Carrick-on-Suir and Waterford	10 July 1850 9&10 5 photocopy	1 2 0 4 5 0 0 0 CL
Kilkenny	Carrick-on-Suir and Waterford [Iverk Barony]	30 December 1850 9&10A 844985 [4] Not in County Library.	0 0 3 0 5 6 0 0 076
Kilkenny	Carrick-on-Suir, New Ross, Thomaston and Waterford	00 October 1850 9&10A	0 0 0 0 0 6 0 0 CL
Kilkenny	Castlecomer, Kilkenny and Thomastown	02 January 1851 9&10A 844985 [4] Not in County Library.	0 0 3 4 5 6 0 0 076
Kilkenny	Castlecomer, Kilkenny and Urlingford	05 October 1850 9&10A 844985 (2)	1 2 3 0 5 6 0 0 074
Kilkenny	Kilkenny	07 July 1849 9&10	1 2 0 0 0 6 0 0 CL

**AN INVENTORY OF THE BOOKS OF SIR RICHARD GRIFFITH'S
GENERAL VALUATION OF RATEABLE PROPERTY IN IRELAND**

County	Poor Law Union	Printing Date Act Remarks Film[Item]	Repository Volume
Kilkenny	Kilkenny	01 August 1849 9&10 Not in County Library.	0 0 0 0 0 6 0 0
Kilkenny	Kilkenny	27 May 1850 9&10A Not in County Library.	0 0 0 0 0 6 0 0
Kilkenny	Kilkenny	03 June 1850 9&10A Not in County Library.	0 0 0 0 0 6 0 0
Kilkenny	Kilkenny and Callan	23 July 1849 9&10	1 2 0 4 0 0 0 0 CL
Kilkenny	Kilkenny and Callan	27 August 1849 9&10	1 2 0 0 0 0 0 0 CL
Kilkenny	Kilkenny and Callan	21 May 1850 9&10A Not in County Library	0 0 0 0 0 6 0 0
Kilkenny	Kilkenny and New Ross	07 February 1850 9&10 5 photocopy. Copy in Wexford CL	1 2 0 4 5 0 0 0 CL
Kilkenny	Kilkenny City	10 May 1849 9&10	0 2 0 4 5 6 0 0 CL
Kilkenny	Kilkenny City	01 November 1850 9&10A 844985 [5]	0 0 3 0 5 0 0 0 CL 077
Kilkenny	New Ross, Thomastown and Waterford	05 October 1850 9&10 101755 [3]	1 2 3 4 5 0 0 0 CL

1-Valuation Office 2-Irish Microforms 3-Family History Library 4-National Library of Ireland
5-National Archives 6-Genealogical Office 7-Dublin Gilbert Library 8-PRONI CL-County Library

**AN INVENTORY OF THE BOOKS OF SIR RICHARD GRIFFITH'S
GENERAL VALUATION OF RATEABLE PROPERTY IN IRELAND**

County	Poor Law Union	Printing Date Act Remarks Film[Item]	Repository Volume
Kilkenny	Urlingford	02 Septemb 1850 9&10A 844985 (3) Not in County Library.	0 0 3 0 5 6 0 0 075
Kings	Edenderry	30 November 1853 15&16 844992 [1]	1 2 3 4 5 0 0 8 CL 122
Kings	Mountmellick	08 February 1851 9&10 101755 [6] CL photocopy	1 2 3 4 5 0 0 0 CL
Kings	Parsonstown	17 August 1854 15&16 844992 [2]	1 2 3 4 5 6 0 0 CL
Kings	Parsonstown and Roscrea	31 May 1851 9&10 SC Not Listed; CL photocopy	1 2 0 4 5 0 0 0 CL
Kings	Roscrea	10 February 1851 9&10 101755 [5] SC Not Listed; CL photocopy	0 2 3 4 0 6 0 0 CL
Kings & Westmeath	Tullamore	01 May 1854 15&16 844992 [3] Copy in Longford/Westmeath CL.	1 2 3 4 5 6 0 8
Leitrim	Ballyshannon	20 February 1857 15&16 844985 (7)	1 2 3 4 5 6 0 0 CL 079
Leitrim	Bawnboy	15 Septemb 1856 15&16 844985 [8] SC 15 December 1856	1 2 3 4 5 6 0 0 CL 080
Leitrim	Carrick-on-Shannon	27 October 1856 15&16 844986 [1]	1 2 3 4 5 6 0 0 CL 081

1-Valuation Office 2-Irish Microforms 3-Family History Library 4-National Library of Ireland
5-National Archives 6-Genealogical Office 7-Dublin Gilbert Library 8-PRONI CL-County Library

AN INVENTORY OF THE BOOKS OF SIR RICHARD GRIFFITH'S
GENERAL VALUATION OF RATEABLE PROPERTY IN IRELAND

County	Poor Law Union	Printing Date Act Remarks Film[Item]	Repository Volume
Leitrim	Manorhamilton	16 March 1857 15&16 844986 [2]	1 2 3 4 5 0 0 0 CL 082
Leitrim	Mohill	30 January 1857 15&16 844986 [3]	1 2 3 4 5 6 0 0 CL 083
Limerick	Croom and Rathkeale	20 December 1850 9&10	1 2 0 4 5 6 0 0 CL
Limerick	Croom, Glin & Rathkeale	20 May 1852 9&10 101755 [8] 2, 3 manuscript,	1 2 3 4 5 0 0 0 CL
Limerick	Croom, Kilmallock, Newcastle and Rathkeale	10 February 1852 9&10 4, 5 photocopy	1 2 0 4 5 0 0 0 CL
Limerick	Croom, Kilmallock & Rathkeale	08 December 1851 9&10 4, 5 photocopy	1 2 0 4 5 0 0 0 CL
Limerick	Croom, Limerick & Kilmallock	05 March 1851 9&10 844987 [5]	1 2 3 4 5 0 0 0 CL 093
Limerick	Glin, Newcastle and Rathkeale	01 July 1852 9&10 844987 [4] 2, 3, 4 manuscript	1 2 3 4 5 0 0 8 CL 092
Limerick	Kanturk, Newcastle and Rathkeale	09 Septemb 1852 9&10 844986 [8] 2, 3, 4, 5, 6 manuscript	1 2 3 4 5 6 0 0 CL 088
Limerick	Kilmallock	18 November 1850 9&10 5 photocopy	1 0 0 0 5 0 0 0 CL

1-Valuation Office 2-Irish Microforms 3-Family History Library 4-National Library of Ireland
5-National Archives 6-Genealogical Office 7-Dublin Gilbert Library 8-PRONI CL-County Library

AN INVENTORY OF THE BOOKS OF SIR RICHARD GRIFFITH'S
GENERAL VALUATION OF RATEABLE PROPERTY IN IRELAND

County	Poor Law Union	Printing Date Act Remarks Film[Item]	Repository Volume
Limerick	Kilmallock	24 May 1851 9&10A 844987 [1] Not in County Library.	0 2 3 4 5 6 0 0 089
Limerick	Kilmallock, Limerick and Tipperary	01 February 1851 9&10 844986 [6]	1 2 3 4 5 6 0 0 CL 086
Limerick	Limerick	15 February 1851 9&10 844987 [3] SC 1 February 1851	1 2 3 4 5 6 0 0 CL 091
Limerick	Limerick and Croom	09 November 1850 9&10 101755 [7]	1 2 3 4 5 6 0 0 CL
Limerick	Limerick and Tipperary	12 February 1852 9&10 844986 [5]	1 2 3 4 5 6 0 0 CL 085
Limerick	Limerick City	02 Septemb 1850 9&10 844987 [2]	1 2 3 4 0 0 0 0 CL 090
Limerick	Limerick City	05 October 1850 9&10 844987 [2]	1 2 3 4 5 0 0 0 CL 090
Limerick	Limerick City	28 May 1851 9&10A Not in County Library.	0 0 0 4 0 0 0 0
Limerick	Mitchelstown and Kilmallock	21 January 1852 9&10 844986 [7]	1 2 3 4 5 6 0 0 CL 087
Londonderry	Ballymoney (Part of)	09 October 1858 15&16 258754 [1] Not in County Library	0 2 3 4 5 0 0 8

1-Valuation Office 2-Irish Microforms 3-Family History Library 4-National Library of Ireland
5-National Archives 6-Genealogical Office 7-Dublin Gilbert Library 8-PRONI CL-County Library

AN INVENTORY OF THE BOOKS OF SIR RICHARD GRIFFITH'S
GENERAL VALUATION OF RATEABLE PROPERTY IN IRELAND

County	Poor Law Union	Printing Date Act Remarks Film[Item]	Repository Volume
Londonderry	Coleraine (Part of)	19 January 1859 15&16 258754 [2] Not in County Library	0 2 3 4 5 0 0 8
Londonderry	Magherafelt	02 March 1859 15&16 258754 [3] Not in County Library	0 2 3 4 5 0 0 8
Londonderry	Newtownlimavaddy	14 August 1858 15&16 258754 [4] Not in County Library	0 2 3 4 5 0 0 8
Longford	Granard	21 December 1854 15&16 844987 [7] SC 4 December 1854	1 2 3 4 5 6 0 8 095
Longford	Longford	22 November 1854 15&16 844987 [8]	1 2 3 4 5 6 0 0 096
Longford & Westmeath	Ballymahon	10 October 1854 15&16 844987 [6] Copy in Longford/Westmeath CL.	1 2 3 4 5 6 0 0 094
Louth	Drogheda, Town of Drogheda	01 Septemb 1851 9&10 Not in County Library	1 2 0 4 5 0 0 0
Louth & Meath	Ardee	10 January 1854 15&16 844990 [5] SC 10 March 1854	1 2 3 4 5 6 0 0 CL 111
Louth & Meath	Drogheda	12 January 1854 15&16 844990 [7]	1 2 3 4 5 6 0 0 CL 113
Mayo	Ballinrobe	07 March 1857 15&16 844988 [1]	1 2 3 4 5 6 0 0 CL 097

**AN INVENTORY OF THE BOOKS OF SIR RICHARD GRIFFITH'S
GENERAL VALUATION OF RATEABLE PROPERTY IN IRELAND**

County	Poor Law Union	Printing Date Act Remarks Film[Item]	Repository Volume
Mayo	Belmullet	01 June 1855 15&16 844988 [2]	1 2 3 4 5 6 0 0 CL 098
Mayo	Castlebar	26 January 1857 15&16 844988 [3]	1 2 3 4 5 6 0 0 CL 099
Mayo	Claremorris	20 August 1856 15&16 844988 [4]	1 2 3 4 5 6 0 0 CL 100
Mayo	Killala	30 January 1856 15&16 844988 [5]	1 2 3 4 5 6 0 0 CL 101
Mayo	Newport	23 March 1855 15&16 844988 [6]	1 2 3 4 5 6 0 0 CL 102
Mayo	Westport	16 May 1855 15&16 844988 [7]	1 2 3 4 5 6 0 0 CL 103
Mayo & Roscommon	Swinford	15 November 1856 15&16 844989 [3] Not in Roscommon County Library	1 2 3 4 5 6 0 0 CL 106
Mayo & Sligo	Ballina	15 May 1856 15&16 844989 [1] Copy in Sligo County Library	1 2 3 4 5 6 0 0 CL 104
Meath	Celbridge	05 March 1851 9&10A 844990 [4] Electoral Division	1 2 3 4 0 0 0 0 CL 110
Meath	Dunshaughlin	21 January 1854 15&16 844990 [1]	1 2 3 4 5 6 0 0 CL 107

AN INVENTORY OF THE BOOKS OF SIR RICHARD GRIFFITH'S
GENERAL VALUATION OF RATEABLE PROPERTY IN IRELAND

County	Poor Law Union	Printing Date Act Remarks Film[Item]	Repository Volume
Meath	Edenderry	10 May 1854 15&16 844990 [1] SC Not Listed	1 2 3 4 5 6 0 8 CL 107
Meath	Navan	28 August 1854 15&16 844990 [2]	1 2 3 4 5 6 0 0 CL 108
Meath	Oldcastle	28 August 1854 15&16 844990 [3]	1 2 3 4 5 6 0 0 CL 109
Meath	Trim	20 October 1854 15&16 844990 [4]	1 2 3 4 5 6 0 8 CL 110
Meath & Cavan	Kells	25 Septemb 1854 15&16 844990 [8] Not in Cavan County Library.	1 2 3 4 5 0 0 8 CL 114
Monaghan	Carrickmacross	27 February 1861 15&16 844991 [1] Parish listed with E. D. SC 27 April 1861.	1 2 3 4 5 0 0 8 CL 115
Monaghan	Castleblaney (Part of)	06 May 1861 15&16 844991 [2] Parish listed with E. D.	1 2 3 4 5 0 0 8 CL 116
Monaghan	Clones (Part of)	17 January 1861 15&16 258758 [1] Parish listed with E. D. SC 8 August 1862.	1 2 3 4 5 0 0 8 CL 117
Monaghan	Cootehill (Part of)	01 May 1858 15&16 844991 [4]	1 2 3 4 5 0 0 8 CL 118
Monaghan	Monaghan	13 December 1860 15&16 844991 [5] Parish listed with Electoral Division.	1 2 3 4 5 0 0 8 CL 119

**AN INVENTORY OF THE BOOKS OF SIR RICHARD GRIFFITH'S
GENERAL VALUATION OF RATEABLE PROPERTY IN IRELAND**

County	Poor Law Union	Printing Date Act Remarks Film[Item]	Repository Volume
Queens	Abbeyleix	12 August 1850 9&10 101757 [4] Not in County Library	1 2 3 4 5 0 0 0
Queens	Abbeyleix and Mountmellick	20 August 1850 9&10 101757 [6] Not in County Library	1 2 3 4 5 0 0 0 --
Queens	Abbeyleix and Mountmellick	07 December 1850 9&10 101757 [5] Not in County Library	1 2 3 4 5 0 0 0 --
Queens	Abbeyleix, Donaghamore and Mountmellick [Upperwoods Barony]	30 November 1850 9&10 101757 SC 30 March1850; 4 photocopy. Not in CL.	1 2 3 4 5 0 0 0 --
Queens	Abbeyleix & Donaghamore [Claremallagh Barony]	08 October 1850 9&10 101757 [2] Not in County Library	0 2 3 4 5 0 0 0 --
Queens	Athy and Carlow	28 Septemb 1850 9&10 844986 [4] Not in County Library	1 2 3 4 5 0 0 0 -- 084
Queens	Athy and Carlow	31 May 1851 9&10A Not in County Library	0 0 0 4 0 6 0 0 --
Queens	Athy and Mountmellick	30 December 1850 9&10 101757 [9] Not in County Library	1 2 3 4 5 0 0 0 --
Queens	Donaghmore and Mountmellick [Clandonagh Barony]	26 October 1850 9&10 101757 [3] Not in County Library	1 2 3 4 5 0 0 0 --
Queens	Mountmellick	03 February 1851 9&10 101757 [7] Not in County Library	1 2 3 4 5 0 0 0 --

AN INVENTORY OF THE BOOKS OF SIR RICHARD GRIFFITH'S
GENERAL VALUATION OF RATEABLE PROPERTY IN IRELAND

County	Poor Law Union	Printing Date Act Remarks Film[Item]	Repository Volume
Queens	Mountmellick	03 February 1851 9&10 101757 Not in County Library	1 2 3 4 5 0 0 0 --
Queens & Kildare	Carlow	28 Septemb 1850 9&10 101757 [8] Not in Laois and Kildare County Library.	1 2 3 4 5 0 0 0
Roscommon	Athlone	05 July 1855 15&16 844992 [4]	1 2 3 4 5 0 0 0 CL
Roscommon	Ballinasloe	17 December 1855 15&16 844992 [5]	1 2 3 4 5 0 0 0 CL
Roscommon	Boyle	20 April 1858 15&16 844992 [6]	1 2 3 4 5 0 0 0 CL
Roscommon	Carrick-on-Shannon (Part of)	20 February 1858 15&16 844992 [7] SC 20 April 1858	1 2 3 4 5 0 0 0 CL 128
Roscommon	Strokestown	28 April 1857 15&16 844992 [8]	1 2 3 4 5 0 0 0 CL
Roscommon & Galway	Roscommon	06 March 1857 15&16 844983 [2] Not in Galway County Library	1 2 3 4 5 0 0 0 CL 061
Roscommon & Mayo	Castlerea	16 April 1857 15&16 844989 [2] Copy in Mayo County Library.	1 2 3 4 5 0 0 0 CL 105
Sligo	Boyle	20 April 1858 15&16 844993 [1]	1 2 3 4 5 6 0 0 CL 130

1-Valuation Office 2-Irish Microforms 3-Family History Library 4-National Library of Ireland
5-National Archives 6-Genealogical Office 7-Dublin Gilbert Library 8-PRONI CL-County Library

An Inventory of the Books of Sir Richard Griffith's
General Valuation of Rateable Property in Ireland

County	Poor Law Union	Printing Date Act Remarks Film[Item]	Repository Volume
Sligo	Dromore West	13 June 1857 15&16 844993 [4] SC 3 June 1857	1 2 3 4 5 6 0 0 CL 133
Sligo	Sligo	18 January 1858 15&16 844993 [2]	1 2 3 4 5 6 0 0 CL
Sligo	Tobercurry	14 December 1857 15&16 844993 [3]	1 2 3 4 5 6 0 0 CL 132
Tipperary	Borrisokane, Nenagh and Parsonstown	25 February 1852 9&10	1 2 0 4 5 0 0 0 CL
Tipperary	Callan, Carrick-on-Suir, Cashel, Thurles and Urlingford	30 November 1850 9&10 101756 [3] Not in County Library.	1 2 3 4 5 0 0 0
Tipperary	Callan, Cashel, Tipperary and Clonmel	05 October 1850 9&10 101756 [2] Not in County Library.	1 2 3 4 5 6 0 0
Tipperary	Carrick-on-Suir, Clogheen and Clonmel	25 October 1850 9&10 844993 [5] SC 27 October 1850	1 2 3 0 5 6 0 0 CL 134
Tipperary	Cashel and Tipperary	12 November 1850 9&10 884993 [7]	1 2 3 4 5 6 0 0 CL 136
Tipperary	Cashel and Tipperary	27 October 1851 9&10 Not in County Library	1 2 0 0 5 6 0 0
Tipperary	Cashel, Nenagh, Thurles and Tipperary	15 August 1851 9&10 884994 [1]	1 2 3 4 5 6 0 0 CL 138

1-Valuation Office 2-Irish Microforms 3-Family History Library 4-National Library of Ireland
5-National Archives 6-Genealogical Office 7-Dublin Gilbert Library 8-PRONI CL-County Library

AN INVENTORY OF THE BOOKS OF SIR RICHARD GRIFFITH'S
GENERAL VALUATION OF RATEABLE PROPERTY IN IRELAND

County	Poor Law Union	Printing Date Act Remarks Film[Item]	Repository Volume
Tipperary	Clogheen and Clonmel	05 August 1852 9&10 884993 [8] 2, 3, 6 manuscript	1 2 3 0 5 6 0 0 CL 137
Tipperary	Nenagh	29 November 1848 9&10 Not in County Library	1 0 0 0 0 0 0 0
Tipperary	Nenagh	16 August 1850 9&10 844994 [2]	1 2 3 4 5 6 0 0 CL 139
Tipperary	Nenagh	14 May 1850 9&10A Not in County Library	0 2 0 4 5 0 0 0
Tipperary	Roscrea & Thurles	01 April 1851 9&10 884993 [6]	1 2 3 4 5 6 0 0 CL 135
Tipperary	Thurles	16 March 1850 9&10 101756 [1]	1 2 3 4 5 0 0 0 CL
Tyrone	Armagh (part of)	09 April 1860 15&16 258754 [5]	0 2 3 4 5 0 0 8
Tyrone	Castlederg	19 March 1860 15&16 258755 [1]	0 0 3 4 5 0 0 8
Tyrone	Cookstown	14 December 1859 15&16 258755 [2]	0 2 3 4 5 0 0 8
Tyrone	Dungannon	04 April 1860 15&16 258755 [3]	0 2 3 4 5 0 0 8

1-Valuation Office 2-Irish Microforms 3-Family History Library 4-National Library of Ireland
5-National Archives 6-Genealogical Office 7-Dublin Gilbert Library 8-PRONI CL-County Library

AN INVENTORY OF THE BOOKS OF SIR RICHARD GRIFFITH'S
GENERAL VALUATION OF RATEABLE PROPERTY IN IRELAND

County	Poor Law Union	Printing Date Act Remarks	Film[Item]	Repository Volume
Tyrone	Enniskillen (Part of)	05 April 1860 15&16	258755 [4]	0 2 3 4 5 0 0 8
Tyrone	Gortin	06 Septemb 1859 15&16	258755 [5]	0 2 3 4 5 0 0 8
Tyrone	Lowtherstown (Irvinestown post 1861)	13 April 1860 15&16	258755 [6]	0 0 3 4 5 0 0 8
Tyrone	Omagh	20 February 1860 15&16	258755 [7]	0 2 3 4 5 0 0 8
Tyrone	Strabane (Part of)	22 November 1858 15&16	258756 [1]	0 2 3 4 5 0 0 8
Tyrone & Monaghan	Clogher	16 January 1860 15&16	258758 [2]	1 2 3 4 5 0 0 8 -- 120
Waterford	Clonmel	18 July 1850 9&10	844994 [6]	0 0 3 4 5 6 0 8 CL 143
Waterford	Clonmel and Carrick-on-Suir	14 May 1850 9&10	844994 [8]	1 2 3 4 5 6 0 0 CL 145
Waterford	Dungarvan and Youghal	02 June 1851 9&10 844994 [4] Not in County Library.		1 2 3 0 5 6 0 0 141
Waterford	Dungarvan, Lismore and Kilmacthomas	19 April 1851 9&10 844994 [5] Not in County Library.		1 2 3 0 5 6 0 0 142

1-Valuation Office 2-Irish Microforms 3-Family History Library 4-National Library of Ireland
5-National Archives 6-Genealogical Office 7-Dublin Gilbert Library 8-PRONI CL-County Library

AN INVENTORY OF THE BOOKS OF SIR RICHARD GRIFFITH'S
GENERAL VALUATION OF RATEABLE PROPERTY IN IRELAND

County	Poor Law Union	Printing Date Act Remarks Film[Item]	Repository Volume
Waterford	Lismore and Youghal	15 Septemb 1851 9&10 844994 [3]	1 2 3 0 5 6 0 0 CL 140
Waterford	Waterford	02 November 1848 9&10 Not in County Library.	1 2 0 4 5 6 0 0
Waterford	Waterford	26 May 1848 9&10 SC not listed. Not in Barony Index or Co.	0 2 0 4 0 0 0 0
Waterford	Waterford	24 April 1849 9&10A 844994 [6]	0 0 3 0 5 6 0 0 CL 143
Waterford	Waterford and Kilmacthomas	20 November 1850 9&10 844994 [7]	1 2 3 4 5 6 0 0 CL 144
Waterford	Waterford City	12 February 1851 9&10 844994 [9]	1 2 3 4 5 6 0 0 CL 146
Waterford	Waterford City	05 Septemb 1851 9&10A Not in County Library.	0 0 0 4 0 0 0 0
Westmeath	Athlone (Part of)	21 August 1854 15&16 844995 [1]	1 2 3 4 5 0 0 0 CL 147
Westmeath	Granard (Part of)	27 June 1854 15&16 844987 [8]	1 2 3 4 5 0 0 0 CL 095
Westmeath	Mullingar	06 December 1854 15&16 844995 [2]	1 2 3 4 5 0 0 8 CL

1-Valuation Office 2-Irish Microforms 3-Family History Library 4-National Library of Ireland
5-National Archives 6-Genealogical Office 7-Dublin Gilbert Library 8-PRONI CL-County Library

AN INVENTORY OF THE BOOKS OF SIR RICHARD GRIFFITH'S
GENERAL VALUATION OF RATEABLE PROPERTY IN IRELAND

County	Poor Law Union	Printing Date Act Remarks	Film[Item]	Repository Volume
Westmeath & Meath	Castletowndelvin	23 June 1854 15&16	844990 [6]	1 2 3 4 5 0 0 0 CL 112
		Copy in Meath County Library		
Wexford	Enniscorthy and Shillelagh (Part of)	17 Septemb 1853 15&16	844995 [3]	1 2 3 0 5 6 0 0 CL 149
Wexford	Gorey	05 July 1853 15&16	844995 [4]	1 2 3 4 5 6 0 0 CL 150
Wexford	New Ross	14 April 1853 15&16	844995 [5]	1 2 3 4 5 6 0 0 CL
Wexford	Wexford	25 May 1853 15&16	844996 [1]	1 2 3 4 5 6 0 0 CL 152
Wicklow	Baltinglass (Part of)	07 January 1854 15&16	844996 [2]	1 2 3 4 5 0 0 0 153
		Copy in Wexford County Library		
Wicklow	Nass	12 October 1853 15&16	844996 [3]	1 2 3 4 5 0 0 0
Wicklow	Rathdown	02 February 1852 9&10	844996 [4]	1 2 3 4 5 0 0 0 155
Wicklow	Rathdrum	05 April 1854 15&16	844996 [5]	1 2 3 4 5 0 0 0 156
Wicklow	Shillelagh (Part of)	17 November 1853 15&16	844996 [6]	1 2 3 4 5 0 0 0

1-Valuation Office 2-Irish Microforms 3-Family History Library 4-National Library of Ireland
5-National Archives 6-Genealogical Office 7-Dublin Gilbert Library 8-PRONI CL-County Library